Celebrate! II

THE ANNUAL FOR CAKE DECORATORS

EDITED BY EUGENE T. AND MARILYNN C. SULLIVAN

WILTON ENTERPRISES, INC. CHICAGO

Celebrate! II

THE ANNUAL FOR CAKE DECORATORS

CELEBRATE! II is a full year's issues of a fresh, newsworthy magazine, bound in hard covers to make it a permanent addition to your decorating library.

In making our bow with this all-new annual publication at this time, we have an especially important occasion to celebrate: the 200th Anniversary of the founding of the United States of America.

Inspired by the Bicentennial, CELEBRATE! II offers you many patriotic designs for beautiful cakes. We've also created 17 unique cakes which pay tribute to those who came to America, whose skill and energy made it great. We know we have not included every national group. If yours is omitted, it is only for lack of space.

Another group of cakes we think you'll like is labeled "Americana." See the "Flying Cloud", the midwest barn, the "1898 Oldsmobile," and other typically American delights.

We've started a new series of cakes that are really "Quick and Pretty", designed for the busy decorator.

And it's been my special pleasure to continue "Commensense for the Cake Decorator", and share with you some of my solutions to decorating problems.

Last, but far from least, we wish to thank all of you who have participated in the preparation of CELEBRATE! II. Your letters have been stimulating and helpful. As a final word, space in this book did not permit our including patterns for cakes, but these are available in the CELEBRATE! II Pattern Book.

We have enjoyed creating CELEBRATE! II with you, and for you. We hope it gives you many years of pleasure.

Norman Wilton

FIRST EDITION
Library of Congress Catalog Card Number: 75-24148
International Standard Book Number: 0-912696-06-0

CELEBRATE!® II is published annually by Wilton Enterprises, Inc., 833 West 115th Street, Chicago, Illinois 60643. NORMAN WILTON, Publisher; MARILYNN C. SULLIVAN and EUGENE T. SULLIVAN, Co-Editors; MICHAEL NITZCHE, Senior Decorator; MARIE KASON and AMY ROHR, Decorators; BECKY HINES, Decorating Assistant. MARSHA ADDUCI, VIRGINIA COLWELL and HELENE GALE, Copy Editors; SANDY LARSEN and CAROL ZALESKI, Art Assistants. DIANE KISH, Reader's Editor. EDWARD HOIS, Photography; JOHN SULLIVAN, Historical Research.

All recipes tested and checked by Culinary Arts Institute Special consultant: Larry Olkiewicz.

CON-
TENTS

THE CELEBRATION YEAR

9. JANUARY & FEBRUARY. New cakes for a new year. Washington's and Lincoln's words and portraits. Sweet cakes for Valentine's day, showers and weddings. Introducing cakes quick to do, pretty to view.

27. MARCH & APRIL bring in spring! Easter eggs, perfect as jewels. Never-before wild flowers. The first of the "Makers of America" cakes. Children's cakes.

45. MAY & JUNE. A gallery of lovely bridal cakes. The prettiest cakes for Mother and Americana cakes for Dad, decorated with unusual techniques.

73. JULY & AUGUST present proud cakes to honor our country's birthday. Bake a replica of a Popcorn Wagon and a patriotic mirror. An English coronation cake. Flowers that grow in American gardens. More portrait cakes of well-loved presidents, and a stunning cake called "China." A cake decorated in the South African style.

105. SEPTEMBER & OCTOBER bring bright new cakes. Harvest cakes, Halloween cakes, a parade of youngsters' cakes. A fantastic lacy Mantilla cake.

125. NOVEMBER & DECEMBER's joyous holidays! A five page Christmas story. Cakes that keep the customs of Christmas. Americana Thanksgiving cakes. A ravishing Swan Lake cake and an oriental tableau.

COMMONSENSE FOR CAKE DECORATORS

146. NORMAN WILTON gives advice on glorifying cakes with color, improvising borders. He shares a few of the possibilities of simple writing tubes. More down-to-earth tips for more beautiful cakes.

GOOD NEWS FOR READERS

4. Grand prize winners in the Original Cake Contest.
6. Patriotic Cake Contest winners.
7. Shaped Cake Contest winners.
8. Grand Prize winners in the Recipe Contest.
26. Winners in the Holiday Cake Contest.
39. Anniversary Cake Contest winners.
57. Cakes for Men Contest winners.
78. Winners in the Teen Cake Contest.
114. Children's Cake Contest winners.
138. Winners in the Anytime Cake Contest.
97. Monthly winners in the Recipe Contest.

THANKS FOR WRITING

102. News, views and advice from our readers.

HOW THE EXPERTS DO IT

14. Ice Carving: Yasuo Minuuchi shows how to create a sparkling fruit basket.

32. Gum Paste: Josefa Barloco shares the secrets behind the creation of a life-like calla lily.

42. The English-Nirvana Method of Decorating: Michael Nitzsche decorates masterpiece cake.

62. The Australian Method of Decorating: Michael Nitzsche shows step-by-step the decoration of a dainty rose-trimmed cake.

120. Decorating in The Mexican Manner. Marithe de Alvarado displays two cakes, explains the method.

122. Pulled Sugar: Norman Wilton creates a breathtaking wedding cake, and shows how to achieve it.

131. Christmas Candy: Larry Olkiewicz shares recipes and know-how for fabulous Swiss chocolates.

DECORATING FOR PROFIT

71. Advice and experience from readers who sell their decorated cakes.

A BRIDAL BOUQUET

68. How to decorate the lovely wedding and engagement cakes in this book.

THE GREEN BOUTIQUE

90. How to create never-before flowers in icing. How to make pine cones, wheat shocks, ears of corn, mount blooms on wire.

MAKERS OF AMERICA

153. Decorating directions for stunning cakes that honor those who made our country great.

DECORATING KNOW-HOW

94. How to cover cakes in marzipan and fondant, for Australian, English, and South African decorating.

96. Modelling with marzipan. How to make fruits, vegetables, elves and other figures.

158. Cutting and serving charts for wedding and party cakes. Amounts of batter to fill pans of various sizes.

INDEX, page 160

ON THE COVER: a cake that sums up how we feel about our country on its 200th birthday. Directions, page 97.

CELEBRATE! II

IS PLEASED

TO PRESENT THE

GRAND PRIZE WINNERS

IN THE

Original Design CAKE CONTEST

These entries were chosen by a
panel of professional decorators,
baking specialists and artists from
hundreds of excellent designs.
Our congratulations to the winners and
sincere thanks to all contestants.

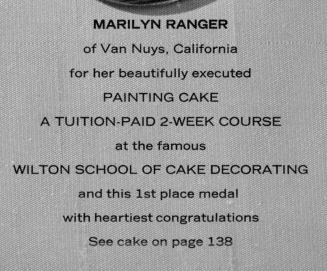

1st PRIZE

MARILYN RANGER
of Van Nuys, California
for her beautifully executed
PAINTING CAKE
A TUITION-PAID 2-WEEK COURSE
at the famous
WILTON SCHOOL OF CAKE DECORATING
and this 1st place medal
with heartiest congratulations
See cake on page 138

2nd PRIZE

3rd PRIZE

NORMA BAILEY

of Bethalto, Illinois

for her appealing

YELLOW DUCK CAKE

A $100

WILTON GIFT CERTIFICATE

and this 2nd place medal

with heartiest congratulations

See cake on page 114

MABEL CROWN

of Rockeville, Maryland

for her highly unique

ALTAR WEDDING CAKE

A $50

WILTON GIFT CERTIFICATE

and this 3rd place medal

with heartiest congratulations

See cake on page 138

Patriotic Cake

CONTEST WINNERS

FIRST PRIZE of $100 and a ribboned medal was awarded to **Arlene Evans** of Waretown, New Jersey for her flag-draped Betsy Ross cake. Arlene decorated "Betsy" with stars and ruffles. The tube 14 star-covered flag was made on a piece of clear plastic wrap cut to the size of the flag (CELEBRATE! II pattern available). Then, while the icing was wet, Betsy's arms were propped with forks stuck into the skirt, and the flag was draped over them to complete this star-spangled winner! Unique and original!

2ND PRIZE of $50 and a ribboned medal was awarded to **Trudy and Dan Cleveland** of Houston, Texas. This clever husband-and-wife team made a "Bike-centennial" cake depicting a bike racer as the spirit of '76. The rider's head and upper body were cut from a sheet cake and the wheels were made from two 8" round cakes. The entire cake was covered with tube 19 stars.

3RD PRIZE of $20 and a ribboned medal was awarded to **Darlene Morton** of Orange Park, Florida for her Boston Tea Party cake. The cup is a dome-trimmed, inverted Wonder Mold. Darlene used a flan pan for her saucer, but we used a 14" base bevel pan. The saucer and card-board handle were decorated with tube 18 stars and the tea cup topped with tinted piping gel. Sugar cube tea boxes and sailing ship were set atop this patriotic winner.

HONORABLE MENTIONS

Three clever cakes win $5.00 gift certificates. **Sylvia Spencer** of Boise, Idaho created a covered wagon with a loaf cake for the base, half-round cakes for the cover and 4" cookies for the wheels.

Dawn Murati of New York decorated a colorful cake banner. She traced a 13-star flag and an eagle onto a two-mix cake then decorated the flag with stars and the eagle with tube 65 "feathers".

Mrs. Darold Ertz of Winner, South Dakota decorated a scene of Mount Rushmore. She made the presidents' faces in Color-Flow, and finger-painted sky and mountains.

PRESENTING THE

Shaped Cake

CONTEST WINNERS

FIRST PRIZE of $100 and a beribboned CELEBRATE! II medal to **Mrs. Leroy McCann** of Oxford, Ohio for her truly ingenious Roller Skate cake.

"Foot" part of skates were two 2" slices cut from the end of a 9" x 13" sheet cake. "Toes", wheels and skate stops were cut from a 6" square single layer. "Ankles" were two cakes baked in regular size soup cans, half-filled with batter. Assembled skates were positioned atop decorated sheet cake, secured by dowel rods and gently iced. Tube 4 was used to add stitching, laces, trim and colorful pompons (over icing mounds).

2ND PRIZE of $50 and a ribbon-hung CELEBRATE! II medal was won by **Bari C. Graves** of Lompoc, California for her colorful butterfly cake.

It was formed of 2 pairs of piano cakes placed in opposite directions and 2 mini loaf pans put end-to-end for body between them. Top piano cakes were carved slightly smaller for true butterfly proportions. Wings and body designs, as well as antennae were made in Color Flow, using Bari's own design.

Leonard Rauch of Fort Lauderdale, Florida, wins THIRD PRIZE and $20. for his unique Compote Cake. He used one half of a Ball cake, flat side down for the base, and the other half, flat side up, for the bowl of the compote, the two connected with a ½" dowel. A petite heart ornament plate supports the bowl. Leonard heaped the compote with colorful marzipan fruit and trimmed it with star tube scrolls. An attractive centerpiece and dessert in one!

HONORABLE MENTION

Theresa Desmond of Wassaic, N.Y., wins $5.00 and our congratulations for her entry. She made a life-like mallard duck of two Egg pan cakes, trimmed and shaped. Cut-off pieces shaped duck's head, and a separately-piped bill of royal icing inserted. Then the iced and outlined duck was filled in with more stars. Theresa used soft natural colors for a striking effect.

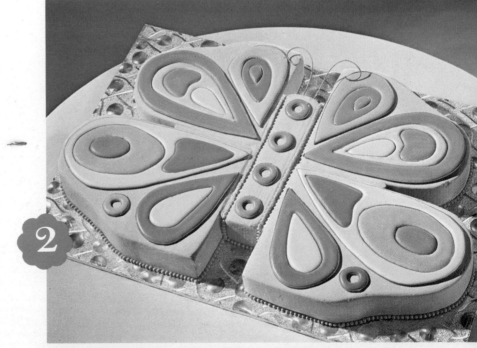

Cake decorated by Valerie Wozney

7

RECIPE CONTEST
Grand Prize Winners

1ST PRIZE

A CHECK FOR $100
AND THIS MEDAL
TO
MARJORIE McDONALD
Panorama City, California

2ND PRIZE

A CHECK FOR $50.00
AND THIS MEDAL
TO
MRS. JEROME DONNELLY
Terre Haute, Indiana

3RD PRIZE

A CHECK FOR $25.00
AND THIS MEDAL
TO
MRS. HOLGER GRAM
Kimball, Nebraska

HERE THEY ARE—the three Grand Prize winners of our six-part recipe contest! Their recipes earned the highest scores over literally thousands of entries.

Expert cooks at the Culinary Arts Institute tested scores of your recipes—then submitted them to a panel of "tasters" for their opinion regarding flavor, appearance and general appeal. Then a group of CELEBRATE! II staff members added their votes. Results were tabulated to determine which dishes received the top scores.

The monthly winners from March through August appear on pages 98 through 101. You'll find the entries of the three Grand Prize Winners there, too.

All the winning recipes were outstanding—and often scores were extremely close. But from them all, these were judged the very best. Congratulations to all winners and special bravos to these three. Warmest thanks to all non-winners, too, all of whom generously shared their excellent recipes with us. We only wish that every excellent recipe submitted could have won a prize.

Celebrate!

THE HAPPY NEW DAYS OF JANUARY & FEBRUARY

Directions for this festive Three Kings centerpiece are on page 66

9

Welcome
TO A New
Year

AN APPROPRIATE BEGINNING for this promising year is our New Year's Cake. This gala gold-and-white centerpiece will bring beauty and good wishes to your New Year's Eve party, New Year's Day dinner or open house celebration.

Every part has a meaning: the heart shaped cake stands for love, the horse-shoe cake for good luck and prosperity. The flowers symbolize hope and fresh beginnings; the candle, the first day of a bright new year; the doves mean peace. The color gold means wealth; and the words "Joy, Peace, Love" bring you and your guests good wishes for the year ahead.

HOW TO DECORATE THE NEW YEAR'S CAKE

In advance, make tube 102 roses and white tube 103 daisies with tube 2 centers. When dry, mount some of the flowers on florist wire.

Bake a 2 layer 15" x 4" heart cake and a horseshoe cake 3" high. Ice cakes smoothly. Place heart cake on gold foil-covered board 1" larger and position horseshoe on top. About halfway between top and bottom of heart cake mark scallops with toothpick and fill with tube 1 cornelli lace to base. (To make lace, using thinned royal icing, pipe many meandering lines of stringwork, zigging and zagging; do not allow lines to touch or cross.

Drape tube 2 stringwork over marked scallops and put a little knot of icing at the point of each scallop. Pipe tube 9 ball border at base and trim each ball with tube 1 stringwork. Drop 3 rows of tube 2 stringwork below top edge of heart and outline lowest row with beading. Pipe a tube 502 shell border around top edge of heart cake.

Next, decorate horseshoe cake. Cover sides with cornelli lace, using tube 1. Pipe tube 501 shell border around the base and tube 8 balls around top, with a tube 1 scroll on each ball.

Pipe tube 1 lettering on both cakes. Anchor tall candle in heart cake, and pipe a mound of icing around it. Trim cake with flowers and add tube 65 leaves. Place two white doves at front of horseshoe. Serves 45 guests.

This jolly cake is dedicated to you, the dedicated decorator! Read how to make it on page 66.

11

A Salute to America's Leaders

Show honor to our country in a very special way with cakes that bear president's words and portraits. Directions for these, and four other Presidential Portrait Cakes in this book start on page 65.

A sparkling sculpture
CARVED IN ICE

HOW THE EXPERTS DO IT
YASUO MIZUUCHI

ICE CARVING is an art that requires considerable practice to produce decorative shapes like the glistening fruit basket on the opposite page—but the results are so spectacular you'll enjoy the work of creating these beautiful centerpieces.

Expert Mr. Yasuo Mizuuchi, Sous Chef at the prestigious Ninety-Fifth Restaurant in Chicago's famous John Hancock Building, is a professional ice carver who has had considerable experience in creating stunning ice sculptures. This basket is a popular shape illustrating basic ice carving techniques and one Mr. Mizuuchi has taught to many of his students.

Here, in pictures and step-by-step directions, you can see just how Mr. Mizuuchi carves a basket of ice. On page 157 you'll find descriptions of the ice carving tools, diagrams of the basket and basics important to any ice carving project.

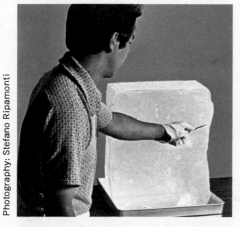

Photography: Stefano Ripamonti

1. The basic outline of the basket is sketched on the ice block with an ice pick.

2. The large-tooth ice saw is then used to cut horizontally into opposite corners of the ice block, exposing a center strip which will be the basket handle. Note how the basket is carved diagonally from corner to corner within the ice block.

3. Now, using a large, flat-edged chisel, the ice is carved away from the sides.

4. Next, using a small ice chisel, the center core of the basket handle is carefully carved out; and then the handle is shaved and smoothed with the same tool.

5. Once again, using the small chisel, the center of the basket is carved out to shape an open inner bowl.

6. Now the large chisel is used to carve ice away from first the top and then the base of the basket, as pictured here, to further define the shape.

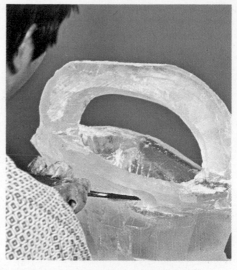

7. With the basket more refined, the small chisel is then used to carve a groove around the top and base of the basket.

8. Again, using the small chisel, vertical grooves are carved into the sides of the basket between the horizontal grooves.

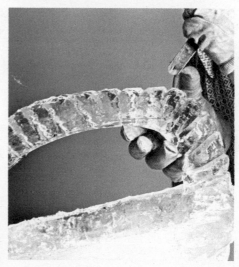

9. Here the small chisel is used to carve the diagonal groove designs around the basket handle; then the same designs are carved within the top and bottom basket rims. The final design is one of alternating rows of diagonal grooves, carved with the small chisel inside the vertical grooves.

15

Pink and Pretty
for
Valentine's
Day

16

A TRIO OF BALLERINAS dance on a ruffled, ribboned, flower-strewn cake.

Make drop flowers using tubes 131, 217 and 225, and 3 shades of pink. Dry.

Bake a 9″ x 4″ petal cake (2 layers) and ice in white. Pipe tube 16 shell border of deep pink around base. Above that pipe 3 rows of tube 104 ruffles in deep pink. Next pipe 3 rows of tube 104 ruffles in lighter pink, and above that 3 rows in pale pink. Above top ruffle pipe a tube 14 zigzag in pale pink. Now drop double row of tube 2 stringwork in deep pink from points of petal, and twirl a knot at each point. Edge top of cake with tube 16 zigzag border. Pipe a tube 16 white fleur-de-lis on

top of cake at point of each petal. Pipe 2 rows of tube 2 scallops on top of cake in deep pink. Then position Dancing Ballerinas in center of cake and pipe tube 1 stems. Place drop flowers and trim with tube 65 leaves. Serves 12.

HEARTS AND ROSES. A frilly, feminine confection—easy to serve, lovely to look at!

Prepare lattice hearts first, using heart cupcake pan as base. Tape pattern for center scroll over back of pan, and tape clear plastic wrap over it, smoothing out wrinkles. To make latticework: use royal icing, drop diagonal lines of tube 2 stringwork starting with longest line and working

up or down from that. Leave center scroll open, and do not extend lines all the way to base; stop about ½″ above base to make removal easier. Then go back to first line, drop stringwork in opposite direction till heart is covered. Pipe tube 14 shell border around base of heart. Pipe tube 14 edge around center scroll. Allow to dry.

Prepare flowers in advance. Make tube 102 roses and rosebuds for top of cake; make tube 67 leaves. When dry, mount leaves and buds on florist wire stems. Make tube 101s roses for bottom border.

Next, bake a 9″ x 13″ x 3″ cake and place on foil-covered board. Ice cake and *Continued on page 66*

Continued on page 66

the Sweetest Cakes for the Prettiest Bride

ROSY ROMANTIC CAKES for the most romantic of seasons and reasons! The heart-shaped engagement party cake subtly forecasts the beauty of the heart-trimmed wedding cake. Directions for both on page 68.

A Victorian Valentine

LOVE DOVES AND CUPIDS,

HEARTS AND TWINING VINES,

A PROFUSION OF BLOSSOMS ON

A LACY BACKGROUND

—ALL MAKE THIS

THE ULTIMATE LOVE CAKE

This sweetly sentimental cake could star as the centerpiece of a very special valentine gathering, announce the engagement of well-loved friends, or even be a most unusual, and wonderful, wedding cake.

Certainly not a quick or easy cake to decorate, but by careful planning, the final assembly will take just a short time. The lavish picture frame, center heart and Color Flow side trims can be made weeks ahead. Then, a day or two before the party, bake and decorate the cake with simple borders and attach the side trims. When the cake is placed in position on the party table, put a number of flat sugar cubes on its top surface and carefully set the picture frame and center heart on the cake.

When it's time to cut the cake, lift off the frame and heart. They can be given as a memento to the honored guest, or saved to glorify another cake!

HOW TO DECORATE

All the Color Flow pattern pieces are made first. To start, tape wax paper over the rectangular-frame pattern and outline it with tube 3 and white Color Flow icing, filling in with blue Color Flow. Let dry completely (preferably overnight), then carefully peel frame off wax paper, invert and repeat outline and fill-in procedure for opposite side. Dry again and cover one side of the blue frame with tube 2 latticework, piping slanted parallel lines of icing in one direction and then overpiping in the opposite direction. Finally trim inner and outer edges of frame with tube 2 white beading. Now set frame aside while you ready the other pattern pieces.

All the heart, large flower, vine, leaf, dove and cupid patterns are done separately, then attached to the frame. Tape patterns to stiff cardboard, then tape wax paper over the cardboard. Outline with tube 2 and fill in with Color Flow icing. Dry thoroughly. Use the same tube for white outer beading around hearts and tube 1 for any tiny inner design beading and trim. Use tube 2 for the white beading around the edges of the corner cupid pattern sections.

Once again, use tube 2 for Color Flow outline and fill-in of the center heart and cake-side patterns. Add white beading around hearts with tubes 1 and 2. When center heart is dry, write message with tube 2.

While all the Color Flow pattern pieces are drying, pipe lots of tiny tube 15 drop flowers, adding center dots with tube 1.

Now decorate the basic frame with the separate Color Flow pieces. Follow the picture for placement, mounding each piece on icing for a raised dimensional effect. Let some of the flowers overlap one another. When all Color Flow pieces are in place, trim with drop flowers, attaching each with a dot of icing. Pipe the bunches of grapes with tube 3, trim the drop flowers with tube 65s leaves, and the Color Flow flowers with tube 67 leaves. Trim Color Flow side pieces with drop flowers and tube 65s leaves also.

Finally, add tiny red hearts with tube 3. Let dry.

Bake a 12" x 18" x 4" high sheet cake. Set on foil-covered board trimmed with Tuk-N-Ruffle. Ice smoothly, then edge base with tube 5 blue balls, and tube 8 white balls. Use tube 5 for top border. Attach Color Flow side trims with dots of icing.

Place flat sugar cubes on top of cake and carefully set "picture frame" and center heart on cake. Your Victorian vision is complete!

Yields 28 to 32 party-size portions, or 90 wedding cake slices.

A QUARTET OF PRETTY LOVE CAKES

Romance is in the air when you serve these attractive hearts-and-flowers cakes. Marvelous for a shower, engagement party, anniversary or a sweetheart's birthday. They're as easy as they are elegant.

These are "Quick & Pretty" Cakes, easy to put together but not beginner-simple. We'll show more of them in later pages. Some have do-ahead decorations, or save time by the use of ready-made plastic trims. There's a graceful hexagon that has each panel framed with a plastic lattice heart, iced and rose-trimmed. The single heart cake, with its simple borders, features a lovable Angelino nestled on top, and the double hearts wear a posy of quick-to-make drop flowers. The ice cream sandwiches can be baked, decorated with buttercream and assembled days ahead, and stored in the freezer; or you can prepare the cookies and add ice cream at serving time.

Part of the Wilton philosophy is the use of legitimate shortcuts and helpers, since we believe you should try to make your cakes as attractive as possible without undue drudgery. Using careful planning, good basic techniques and these aids, you can achieve maximum beauty with "Quick & Pretty" cakes.

SWEETHEART ICE CREAM SANDWICHES

Have these ready in your freezer as a sweet surprise for Valentine-time or any time you want to show someone how much you care.

In advance, make a number of tube 225 drop flowers in pink and yellow.

Next, bake cookies of your favorite light-colored dough shaped with Big Hearted Cookie Cutter. When cooled, decorate cookies with simple designs, using tube 2 for strings and dots, tube 13 for star borders. Trim some cookies with clusters or borders of drop flowers attached with icing. Pipe tube 65 leaves on flowers. For heart design on cookie, outline with tube 2 and fill in with regular (not Color Flow) icing. Leave an equal number of the cookies un-iced.

Now, shape softened strawberry or cherry ice cream in heart cupcake pans and freeze until firm. Assemble a plain heart cookie, ice cream, and decorated cookie, and serve.

VALENTINE POSY

A sweet double heart cake, crowned with an old-fashioned nosegay!

In advance, make tube 131 and 194 drop flowers in gay-colored royal icing. Make leaves with tube 70. When dry, mount flowers and leaves on florist wire. (See page 90.)

Bake two 1-layer heart cakes, 9" x 2" and 6" x 2", and ice tops pink and sides white. Assemble on heart-shaped board edged with pink Tuk-N-Ruffle. Pipe tube 19 pink shell border around base of lower tier, and tube 17 white shell border around base of upper tier. Pipe tube 14 border in scallop design around top edges of both tiers, and drop a tube 14 star at point of each scallop.

To make posy, shape small paper doily into cone and snip point. Arrange flowers and leaves in a cluster, twist stems together, and insert into cone. Secure with royal icing. Add a ribbon bow. Place some flowers on lower tier for accent. Serves 9.

HEART SEXTET

Six lacy, rose-trimmed hearts frame this pretty centerpiece cake that's iced in softest peach.

In advance, make tube 103 wild roses in shades of pink, with yellow centers. "Paint" plastic Filigree Hearts with thinned white icing. Allow to dry.

Bake and ice a 2-layer 9" hexagon cake. Pipe white tube 19 reverse shell border around base of cake. Now attach a wild rose in center of each Filigree Heart and trim with tube 67 leaves; position a heart at each angle of cake and secure with dots of icing. Set two wild roses with leaves in border at tip of each heart. Insert candle in center of cake, pipe mound of icing around it and cover with wild roses. Pipe tube 67 leaves. 12 generous servings.

ANGEL FACE

A smiling little angel spreads his wings on this charming love cake.

First make a supply of tube 225 drop flowers in shades of pink. Let dry.

Next, bake a 9" x 4" heart cake and a heart cupcake, and ice both pink. Place on serving plate. Fill in sides of cake with tube 1 cornelli lace. (See page 10.) Pipe tube 12 white ball border around base of cake and tube 8 ball border around top edge of cake.

Position heart cupcake in center of larger cake. With toothpick, make a heart-shaped guideline about 1¼" out from bottom edge of cupcake. Pipe tube 3 beading around bottom edge of cupcake, then drop tube 2 white stringwork from top edge of cupcake to guideline. Finish with tube 2 beading to cover guideline. Pipe mound of icing on cupcake and position Angelino, then trim with a cluster of drop flowers. Pipe tube 65 leaves. Serves 12.

CONGRATULATIONS, YOU WON!
A parade of stunning holiday cakes

Our creative readers sent in a wide variety of new and appealing holiday cakes for this contest. There were fresh ideas on every holiday theme in the calendar, from New Year's to the 4th of July—and on to Christmas. Here are the winners.

FIRST PRIZE and a $25 Gift Certificate to **Karen Ramsay,** Hinkley, California for her lovely Martha Washington cake. Karen baked the skirt in the Wonder Mold and spread icing thickly over it, then formed folds with a spatula. Tube 104 flounces edged the skirt. The overskirt was piped with tube 32 shells. Bodice was filled in with small stars and puff sleeves with tube 14.

We followed Karen's directions for the elaborate hairdress. Trim off the doll's hair and create the "piled-up" effect with tube 362. Thirteen tube 4 ringlets finished the coiffeur.

An elegant patriotic doll to celebrate the Bicentennial, or any patriotic holiday!

SECOND PRIZE and a $15 Gift Certificate goes to **Gay Briand,** St. Catherine's, Ontario, who dreamed up this darling Christmas Stocking. Gay built the stocking from five 6" round cakes, filled and stacked. The "toe" is formed from two oval cakes, filled and trimmed to 3" height. The ovals

are trimmed in a curve to fit partly around the 6" cakes. Stars all over and a fluffy tube 30 cuff trim the stocking. Brightly-decorated "toy" cookies and candy canes finish it off. This cake was the star attraction of her daughter's Christmas party.

THIRD PRIZE and a $10 Gift Certificate was won by **Karen Cvetko,** Northbrook, Illinois, from this unique Thanksgiving Turkey Cake.

Karen used three cakes to form her turkey, baked in the Clown Pan, the small Wonder Mold and a half Ball. The Ball cake forms his breast, placed on the forehead area of the Clown cake. Just above it, she placed the Wonder Mold cake for his head, trimming it a little, so it fit snugly into the Ball cake. The cake was iced smoothly to eliminate humps in the Clown pan, then covered with bright stars. Bright blue eyes and a scarlet wattle, piped with tube 16, completed a perky Tom Turkey.

HONORABLE MENTION

Mary Cleveland of Falls Church, Virginia, wins a $5 Gift Certificate for her sweet little Pilgrim doll cake, made with the Wonder Mold. She wears a soft brown dress and bonnet, both trimmed in white, and a crisp white apron. Mary made a tiny broom from a twig and clippings from her kitchen broom for the Pilgrim Miss to hold.

Cake decorated by Valarie Wozney

Celebrate!

THE ARRIVAL OF SPRINGTIME IN MARCH & APRIL

Read how to make these fabulous ''Faberge'' eggs on page 67

A Welcome to Spring

Spring is the season of hope and of fresh beginnings, the time for some of our happiest holidays. Winter's chill is gone, flowers are emerging and trees are budding. It's a glorious season of life's renewal, and a delightful time for parties.

IRELAND

This delicate shamrock-wreathed wedding cake was decorated to honor our Irish ancestors—and to pay special tribute to a bride of Irish descent.

As early as 1798, large groups of Irish came to the new world following an unsuccessful rebellion.

In the hundred years from 1820 to 1920, four and a quarter million Irish had settled in America. By 1850, the Irish replaced the English as our chief source of settlers—making up 44% of the foreign-born population.

They came with dauntless optimism and spirit to escape famine and hardship in their native country. They remained to build our towns and factories, to help stretch 30,000 miles of railroad across the continent, to teach our children and to govern many cities. Irish wit and laughter, song and deep religious devotion are part of the very texture of American life.

Directions for decorating the lovely "Happy Spring" cake below are on page 66. Decorating directions for "Ireland", page 153.

IRELAND

MAKERS
of
AMERICA

Capture the color of spring in

America's dainty wild flowers

MANY FLOWER LOVERS throughout America appreciate the delicate beauty of wild flowers in their natural settings. Now you can capture this beauty in icing. Trillium, golden Marsh Marigolds, Spring Beauties and Blue Bellflowers can all be artfully arranged on cakes to achieve small, elegant showpieces.

DECORATING THE CAKES

Make all of the wild flowers you intend to use well in advance, Mount most of your blooms on green florist wire, to provide greater flexibility in decorating. Let flowers, as well as leaves, where used, dry thoroughly before arranging. These cake designs are purposely uncomplicated to emphasize the appealing colors and shapes of the wild flowers. Directions for making flowers are on page 90.

TRILLIUM CAKE. Bake an 8″ x 3″ round cake and ice in pale apricot. Pipe tube 4 bulb border around base, with tube 4 beading and half scallops around top. Display Trillium blossoms and leaves to suit your taste. Serves 10.

MARSH MARIGOLD CAKE. Ice an 8″ x 3″ square cake a dainty green. Pipe a tube 3 bulb border around base and a border of tube 3 scallops around top. Arrange wired Marigolds on cake in an informal spray and continue with unwired blooms at base. Serves 12.

SPRING BEAUTY CAKE. Bake a 9″ x 3″ heart cake and ice with pastel pink buttercream icing. Pipe green tube 2 beading around base and then arrange flowers and leaves tastefully in and next to this border. Insert a mini-bouquet of wired Spring Beauties in center of cake. Serves 12.

OVAL WILD FLOWER CAKE. To achieve this gem of the decorator's art, bake a two layer oval cake and ice white. Mark curving line from base to 1″ below top of cake, dropping again to base. Fill in space between mark and base of cake with tube 3 latticework. Pipe scrolls with tube 7. Pipe tube 17 shell border around base and cover top with tube 3 latticework. Next pipe tube 17 shell border around top edge. Pipe mounds of icing and position garlands of flowers around base and top. Serves 12.

Opposite page: far left, Trillium cake; top left, cake adorned with yellow Marsh Marigolds; bottom left, Spring Beauties bloom on a heart cake. Cake below trimmed with Trillium, Marsh Marigolds and Spring Beauties, further embellished with Blue Bellflowers.

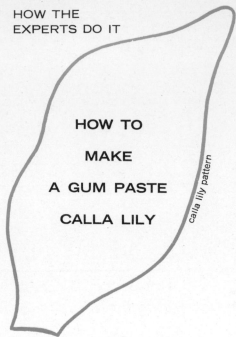

calla lily pattern

HOW TO MAKE A GUM PASTE CALLA LILY

AS TAUGHT BY JOSEFA BARLOCO

A long-time admirer of the beauty of flowers, Josefa Barloco has created a garden of gum paste for party and cake decorating. Mrs. Barloco, a recognized expert in the art of gum paste, reproduces flower varieties petal by petal to capture the loveliness of nature. Here, her calla lily, one of the easiest and most beautiful flowers to make, is illustrated step-by-step.

GUM PASTE RECIPE

1 tablespoon Wil-tex™ or
    Tragacanth gum
1 heaping teaspoon glucose
3 tablespoons warm water
1 tablespoon lemon juice
1 pound powdered sugar (or more)

Mix warm water and glucose until glucose is absorbed. Add the gum and lemon juice and, when thoroughly mixed, add small amounts of powdered sugar until you can work the mixture with your hands. Continue adding small amounts of powdered sugar as you knead the mixture on a table top. As soon as the mixture is pliable and can be shaped without sticking to your fingers, you've added enough sugar and the gum is of working consistency.

HOW TO HANDLE GUM PASTE

Always dust your work surface with cornstarch first! Then, take a small piece of gum paste, work it awhile with your hands and place it on the cornstarch-covered area. Dust the surface of your hands and rolling pin with cornstarch, and roll out the gum paste to the thickness you desire. Always roll out one piece of gum paste at a time and cover every flower petal you make to avoid drying.

Note: if you're not going to use the gum paste immediately, store it in a plastic bag inside a covered container. It will keep for several months, but you will need to rework it with your hands until soft.

MAKING THE CALLA LILY

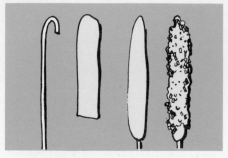

Make stamen first. Fold one end of a six-inch length of florist wire ¼-inch do as shown. Dip this fold in egg white and insert it into an elongated piece of yellow-tinted gum paste. (Use food color to tint gum paste, adding small amounts with a toothpick.) Now roll gum paste until it's about two inches long, brush with egg white, roll in crystal sugar and set in styrofoam to dry.

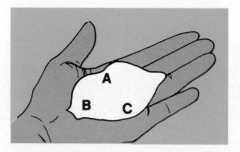

Cut out flower. Dust work surface with cornstarch and roll out gum paste to 1/16-inch thickness. Use the pattern and a sharp knife to cut out the petal, then placing it point forward on your palm, brush egg white from point A to point B.

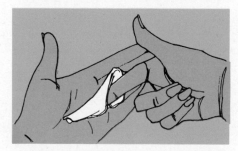

Overlap petal. Fold petal side AB to overlap side C, using your fingers to press the two sides together until joining seam is smooth.

Curl the petal. Place the flower over the point of a paper cone cup and, with your fingers, fold the petal edges back. Let dry.

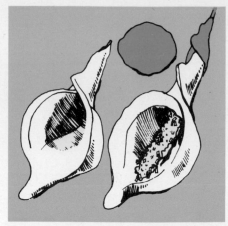

Brush the throat. After the flower has dried, use an artist brush to paint the inner throat with dry yellow tempera color. This sunny color gives the calla lily its true personality.

Add the stamen. Brush egg white around the base of the stamen and insert wire end into flower, pulling the wire through until the stamen is in place. Now wrap a green-tinted piece of gum paste around the flower base and set in styrofoam to dry.

ASSEMBLE BOUQUET

To make the stunning bouquet shown on the opposite page, you will need 1½-inch wide, non-woven yellow satin ribbon, 3-inch wide yellow tulle, 6-inch florist wires, green florist tape and five calla lilies.

Begin the arrangement by wrapping the flower bases with green florist tape. Next, make the net butterflies. Cut net tulle into half-yard lengths; then take one piece at a time and gather net together at center with your fingers. Place a wire behind the net and fold one end tightly over the gathered center without twisting the wire. Now, start taping flowers and net butterflies together one by one, staggering the heighths as you tape.

Completed, your calla lily corsage is ready to become an admired party cake decoration, one that will be treasured as a birthday, anniversary or engagement keepsake! Whatever the occasion, gum paste flowers make it extra special.

If you would like to know more about this fascinating art, you would truly enjoy our latest book, "The Wilton Way of Making Gum Paste Flowers as taught by Josefa Barloco. 64 full-color pages with step-by-step instructions for making breathtaking gum paste flowers as well as mint sugar party trims. Fabulous gum paste flower cakes, bouquets and table centerpieces, even a corsage of orchids! Cutters, tools and ingredients available, too.

DECORATE A CALLA LILY CAKE

This picture shows how a simply-decorated cake can become breathtakingly lovely with a trim of gum paste flowers. Practice until you can create the calla lily spray— then decorate this cake for the highlight of a very special spring luncheon or tea. The guest of honor may be given the flower spray as a lasting memento.

Bake a 10" x 3" square cake (two layers) and ice pale yellow. Place on gold foil-covered board trimmed with yellow Tuk-N-Ruffle. Pipe tube 17 yellow shell border around base of cake. Pipe 17 green scrolls around lower part of cake just above bottom border and overpipe with an "e" motion. Pipe tube 17 white scrolls around top portion just below top of cake and overpipe with an "e" motion. Add a white scroll at each corner on top of cake with same tube. Accent scrolls with tube 4 dots. To complete the cake, position spray of lilies on top.

A SALUTE TO

THOSE WHO MADE OUR COUNTRY GREAT

OVER THREE CENTURIES AGO settlers from two far-flung continents—Europe and Africa—made their way to the homeland of the American Indian, little realizing their descendants would be among the "makers of America".

AFRICA

A rich heritage of African art, handicrafts and folklore is being discovered these days all throughout America. Many of the ancestors of black American families are reported to have landed at Jamestown as early as 1619, very shortly after the arrival of the early English settlers. Most came from a 3,000-mile stretch of the West African coast, bringing with them a varied richness of customs and legends. Our African cake draws on this background. It uses natural colors, the tones of the earth and sky, arranged in a geometric design of lines and circles reminiscent of the decoration of African tribal masks and native textiles.

AMERICAN INDIAN

The American Indians, truly the earliest settlers of modern day America, adapted nature's most familiar forms—sun, moon, bird and flower—into their pottery, textiles and even jewelry. Here stylized designs of the sun and eagle, plus the colors of sky, sun and sand, have been used to make this uniquely American Indian Thunderbird cake.

HOLLAND

This Delft-trimmed wooden shoe cake filled with bright tulips makes an enchanting centerpiece for a springtime luncheon or party. It is a tribute to the sturdy Dutch who came to "Nieu Amsterdam" in 1623. Later, hundreds of thousands of their thrifty industrious countrymen emigrated to America and settled in Pennsylvania, Michigan, Wisconsin, Iowa and many other areas in the new world. Hearty, delicious foods, a passion for neatness and cleanliness, and the brilliant tulip are just three of their contributions to America. Throughout the country many of their descendants still hold colorful annual festivals when tulips are in bloom.

Directions for decorating these "Makers of America" cakes start on page 153.

MAKERS of AMERICA

A very special Easter treat

EASTER IS A JOYOUS TIME FOR CHILDREN OF ALL AGES

THREE-D LAMB

Bake cake in stand-up Lamb Pan. To decorate, outline eyes, ears, nose and mouth with tube 3. Fill in eyes and inside of ears with softened Color Flow icing. When eyes and ears are dry, brush with corn syrup to give a nice shine. Outline feet and bow-tie. Pipe tube 16 stars to fill in face, bow-tie and feet. Pipe additional stars to build up cheeks and nose.

Fluff effect on lamb's coat is made with tube 12 using half "C" motion. Serves 12.

Do your Easter decorating with children in mind. From babyhood to teen-age (and beyond), everyone is delighted with tastefully-designed Eastertime cakes. Create a traditional blue-eyed woolly lamb cake. Or go a bit more whimsical and fashion a storybook centerpiece like The Old Woman Who Lived In a Shoe. This edible adaptation of the classic nursery rhyme is a-sparkle with color and alive with cookie figures that represent the many children who lived in the shoe.

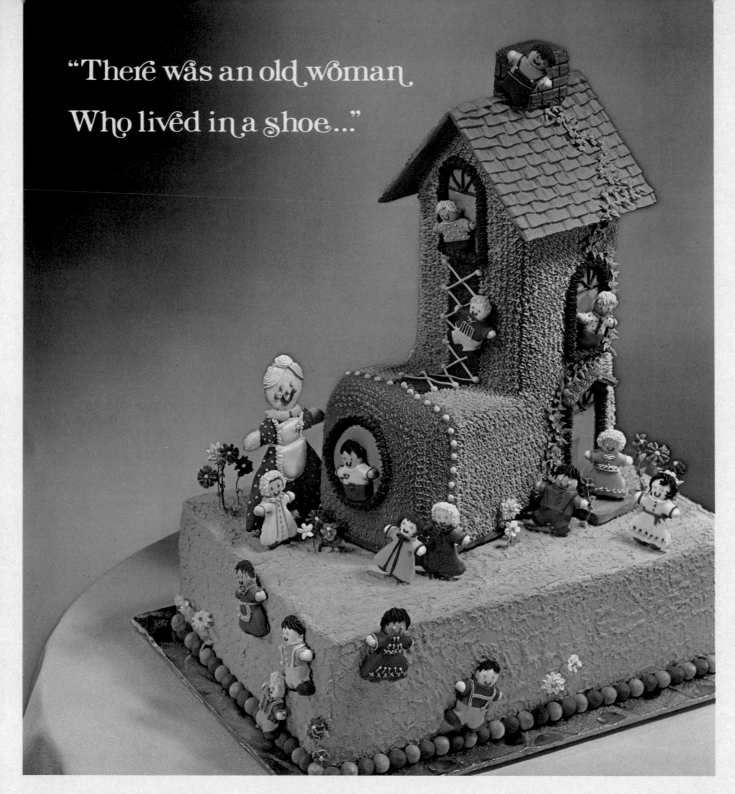

"There was an old woman Who lived in a shoe..."

OLD WOMAN IN SHOE CAKE

First, make tube 217 and 225 drop flowers and mount some on wire. Then make a number of boy and girl cookies using gingerbread cutters. Ice and trim with tube 2 lines and dots. Bake a large cookie for the Old Woman, ice and trim with tube 2 hair, eyes, nose and mouth. For her apron, use Color Flow method; outline with tube 2, flow in color and add tube 2 beading around edge. Scatter tube 1 dots on dress.

For base, bake a 9"x13" two-layer cake and ice green; pat lightly with sponge for all-over stucco effect. Place on green foil covered board. Pipe tube 12 ball border around base of cake. To make the house: bake cake in 16"x4" loaf pan. When it has cooled, cut in half. One half is the base of the house; trim one end for toe. Measure other half and cut 5" oblong for the upright section and 4"x3" triangle for peak of roof.

Assemble "shoe house" on board cut to fit: insert dowels in base to support upright section. Place more dowels between upright section and roof triangle. Ice the house pink. Outline all windows and door with tube 2, and flow in blue thinned Color Flow icing. Outline strip down front of shoe. When windows are dry, glaze with corn syrup.

Pipe tube 2 stars to fill in shoe, toe, window frames, and strip down front. Pipe tube 5 extension over door, topped with tube 16 zigzag. Cut thin cardboard to make roof; fold in half, and ice orange, using tube 45 to make shingle effect. Start at bottom of roof and work to peak. Fashion chimney from remaining cake, ice deep pink and place on roof. Trace bricks with toothpick. Pipe tube 2 laces down strip in front of shoe. Position cookie boys and girls, and Old Woman figure, supporting with tooth picks and popsicle stick. Place wired flowers and leaves on cake. Pipe tube 65s "vines." Serves 32.

ISRAEL

THE JEWISH PEOPLE have figured prominently in the history of America, both before and after the formation of the United States. Luis de Torres, a Jew, sailed with Columbus on his first voyage and is reputed to have been the first of the crew to step on American soil. In 1654, a group of 23 Jews, under the auspices of the Dutch West India Company, landed in New York (then New Amsterdam), and approximately a century later Touro Synagogue in Newport, Rhode Island, was dedicated.

Beginning as early as 1815, thousands of Jewish families came to the United States from Germany, and during the latter part of the nineteen century and the early part of the twentieth further thousands of Jewish families fled to the U. S. from continuing persecution in Russian dominated territories. All of these settlers brought with them the rich traditions of a centuries-old culture.

We decorated this handsome Star of David cake as a tribute to our Jewish-American citizens. It was suggested to us by a reader, Karen Cvetko. Details start on page 153.

TULIP TIME

Bright tulips trim a patchwork cake to star at spring parties.

Bake and ice two square tiers, 8" x 2" and 12" x 3". Assemble on serving tray. Next, measure off six equal sections on each side of large cake and mark with a tiny dot of icing as a guide. Mark off smaller cake, four sections on each side. Pipe tube 2 stringwork in diamond pattern on top of both cakes, using these guide marks.

Pipe tube 3 stems and tube 65 leaves on sides of both tiers. Then pipe tulips at top of stems using tube 5 and a shell motion. Pipe two pointed petals on either side, then one petal in center. Pipe more tulips on top of tiers, centering in diamond shapes.

Pipe tube 199 shell border at base of 12" tier, tube 17 border at top of tier. Use tube 16 for borders of 8" tier. Center cake with Tulip Party Cup. Mound icing inside cup and set in candle. Serves 44.

CONGRATULATIONS!

YOU WON!

Talented readers have submitted hundreds of charming entries in our Anniversary Cake Contest. We only wish we had the space to show you every one. Here are the winners and their cakes.

PILLOW TALK

First Prize and a $25 Gift Certificate goes to **Mrs. M. Kidd** of McGregor, Texas, for this pretty cake that salutes a 10th wedding anniversary. The top of the cake is strewn with dainty pink daisies, and set off by a scalloped "embroidered" border, accented with piping gel. A Loving Couple is seated in the center. Mrs. Kidd used an 11" x 15" sheet cake.

ANNIVERSARY BELLS

Another talented Texan, **Mrs. H. N. Golden** of Houston, wins a $15 Gift Certificate as Second prize for her sheet cake for a large anniversary party.

Mrs. Golden used two 12" x 18" sheet cakes for her base, but you could vary the size as we did and use 11" x 15" cakes. Two bell-shaped cakes and masses of roses break up the expanse beautifully, and the bell cakes can be given to the guests of honor. (Mrs. Golden places them on cake boards cut the same shape.)

A STAMP OF LOVE

An intriguing story goes with the cake that won Third Prize and a $10 Gift Certificate for **Marion Vandergrift** of Philadelphia. She created this special theme cake for a couple celebrating the 2nd anniversary of their engagement and his entering the service. For two years they wrote each other daily, using the "Love" stamp on every letter. Marion reproduced this stamp on the cake. We have included a Love Stamp Color Flow pattern in CELEBRATE! II Pattern Book that fits a 9" x 13" Cake.

HONORABLE MENTION

Moni Hourt of Crawford, Nebraska, receives a $5 Gift Certificate for her humorous 40th wedding anniversary cake. When the anniversary celebrants were on their honeymoon, the lights of their car went out, and the bride had to sit on the hood of the car holding a flashlight. Mari reproduced this scene with a styrofoam replica of the car and gum paste figures. The car was set on a sheet cake.

Honorable Mention and a $5 Gift Certificate also goes to **Frances O'Brien** of Jordan, N. Y., who created a special 20th Anniversary cake for the Memphis, N. Y. Fire Department. Frances trimmed a 14" square cake for the base and parking area and 3 9" x 13" cakes for the building. All details were included, even to the tower, floodlights and small model trucks.

QUICK & PRETTY

FIVE FRESH NEW IDEAS for cakes that will add color and charm to Springtime parties. All can be put together quickly using basic techniques and plan-ahead trims.

ST. PAT'S HAT. Green as Ireland's grass and a great party centerpiece. Ahead of time make Color Flow buckle, 1¾" x 2" and shamrock flowers and leaves. (Directions start on page 90). Have gum paste ready. (Recipe on page 32.)

Bake three 6" round layers, stack, chill and taper to 5" at top. Cake should be 5" high. Ice and place on 10" foil-covered board. For brim, measure and mark cake ¾" from base. Build up a thick layer of icing on board, and bevel with spatula from marked area to edge of board. Edge

with tube 5 beading.

As soon as icing has set, roll out gum paste, cut a strip about 1½" x 20" and immediately wrap around hat. Let dry. Attach buckle with icing and trim with shamrock flowers and leaves. Serves 10, but is almost too pretty to cut!

EASTER CUPCAKES AND DOUGHNUTS. Delight the children on Easter morning with this colorful surprise.

Have on hand tiny figures (and also picks) of lambs, geese, bunnies and chicks, a supply of tiny drop flowers, and plenty of cupcakes and doughnuts.

Swirl the cupcakes and doughnuts with icing. Edge cupcakes with swags, zigzags, stars or beads—pull out "hay" on doughnuts with tube 233. Place Easter figures and scatter gay drop flowers. Be prepared for cries of delight.

A SHOWER CAKE FOR BABY. Dainty and sweet as the new arrival! Ahead of time, make lots of tube 224 drop flowers, centered with tube 2 dots.

Bake and ice a 10" x 4" round cake. Now, pipe ten strips around side of cake with tube 47, starting each strip at the top. Pipe tube 102 ruffles along both sides of each strip. Add tube 21 shell border around base of cake and tube 18 border around the top. Attach flowers on each

Continued on page 66

AN ENGLISH METHOD MASTERPIECE CAKE

AND ITS PRETTY AMERICAN COUSIN

Directions for decorating this cake on page 66

IN ENGLAND, cake decorating is a very highly-developed art indeed, and English cakes are truly unique. They are distinguished by their geometric shapes and trims, almost architectural in feeling, and by their very formal air.

The typical English celebration cake is fruitcake, covered completely with rolled marzipan and iced to perfect smoothness with a thin coat of royal icing.

Flowers are usually piped of royal icing also, although they are sometimes modelled of marzipan. Borders are piped mainly with a fine writing tube and consist of beads, cornelli lace and linework designs.

There are two distinctive English methods—the Lambeth, that features elaborately overpiped scrollwork and the Nirvana demonstrated here.

The Nirvana method features graceful "run-in" panels and collars for cakes, made with the same techniques as our Color Flow designs, but used in a completely different and beautiful way.

Michael Nitzsche, CELEBRATE! II expert, has created the lovely Nirvana method English cake on the facing page. On this page, we present an American adaptation, achieved in the time-saving Wilton-American way.

HOW TO DO THE RUN-IN PIECES

The correct icing is very important. Use egg-white royal to outline the pieces—then thin the icing with lemon juice for running-in. Color Flow icing is also satisfactory.

Mix the icing by hand to avoid whipping in too much air. After thinning the icing, let it stand for 24 hours to allow any bubbles to come to the surface.

The icing for run-in work should be just thick enough so that it will not run out of a snipped paper cone—but thin enough so a light pressure will cause it to flow.

Using the same technique as for Color Flow work, and Celebrate! II patterns, outline all the pieces with tube 2 and unthinned icing. Then start to run-in with thinned icing.

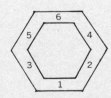

The order of running-in is important to keep a smooth finish on the work. For base collar, upper base collar and top splay, follow the order shown on the diagram. Move quickly so that icing blends.

For the base splay that rests on top of the cake, have two cones filled with icing ready. Mark where the second top splay will extend on your pattern, and use one

continued on page 44

bag of icing to run-in to that point. Follow the order given in the diagram. Then fill in the center area with second cone of icing, working in a spiral to the center.

For the center plaque, start in the middle and move out to edge.

For the side windows, start with the center arch, and then move out to the edges. Keep run-in work thin and flat.

When you have completed running-in the pieces, dry them under a heat lamp, two feet above them, until a crust forms. This gives a glossy finish. Then complete the drying for 48 to 72 hours.

After the pieces are dry, edge the base collar, upper base collar, two top splays and center plaque with beading using tube 3. Let dry again.

Now turn these pieces over and pipe riser lines on reverse sides, following pattern indications. Pipe a line with tube 3, then over-pipe with same tube. Then over-pipe with two lines using tube 2. Dry.

Outline "Amy" (or name of your choice) with tube 2 on center plaque. Overpipe outline again and dry. Brush in thinned icing in lightest shade. Immediately brush in deeper, then deepest color icing to blend. Let dry.

HOW TO ASSEMBLE THE CAKE

1. Make roses and rosebuds with tube 102. Set aside to dry. Pipe stems on wax paper with tube 3 and trim with leaves made with a v-cut cone. Dry.

2. Bake a 8" x 3" round fruit cake. Cover with marzipan, following directions on page 94. Now ice smoothly with royal icing.

3. Prepare the cake board. Use a 16" masonite circle, or four 16" circles of corrugated board taped together, each covered with silver foil. Or use a ready-made silver foil board. Pipe riser lines on board with tube 4, using pattern as guide. Dry.

4. Center cake on board, attaching with a few dots of icing.

5. Slip base collar over cake. Set upper base collar on top of base collar, matching corners of hexagon shape.

6. Set all six windows *on cake board, within base collars*. Adjust to fit. Fix windows to cake at top center with dots of icing.

7. Pipe bead borders with tube 3 at sides, bottom and top of windows to conceal join.

8. Attach stems and leaves to windows with icing. Attach roses and buds *to cake*.

9. Pipe six dots of icing on top of cake and set large splay in position matching angles with base collars.

10. Center top splay on top base splay, matching angles and fixing with dots of icing on risers.

11. Center plaque in same manner.

12. Display with pride! To serve, break the beautiful run-in work with a silver knife.

Celebrate!

ROMANTIC DAYS, LOVING DAYS IN MAY & JUNE

Trim a cake for Mother with ribbons
and polka dots. Directions on page 70

45

Almost as beautiful as the Bride

STARTING HERE, a collection of the loveliest bridal cakes ever gathered together. Cakes trimmed in the grand tradition or sweetly simple, heaped with flowers or lavished with lattice and lace. All can be adapted to the bride's own color scheme—all serve as inspirations for your own creative ideas.

Wedding cakes have always been the special joy of decorators—and we have enjoyed decorating these cakes to show you.

ABOVE: A centerpiece cake for the engagement party or rehearsal dinner. Bright butterflies are its accent. AT RIGHT: The bridal cake adorned with the largest, laciest butterflies ever! Directions for both start on page 68.

Crystal

A sparkling fountain plays
atop a wedding cake of
traditional beauty

Decorating directions start on page 68

48

Decorating directions are on page 154

France

Fleurs-de-lis, the flower of France, accent this striking bridal cake

MAKERS of AMERICA

Lavender

Dainty loops of icing frame a cake
trimmed with sweet simplicity

Decorating directions for both cakes start on page 68

50

Summertime

Loveliest of all, fresh flowers grace
this cake for the summer bride

Garden

Brilliant garden flowers
are heaped on a snow-white cake
festooned with frilly garlands

are cut and put in small boxes for guests to take home, but often they are served at the reception. An iced fruit cake or a chocolate cake are the favorites.

CHOCOLATE GROOM'S CAKE

Bake and fill two-layer 10" square cake and ice with milk chocolate frosting. Use dark chocolate icing for all decorating. Cover the top of the cake with tube 2 lattice, first piping lines parallel to one side of the cake, then diagonally, then in the opposite diagonal direction.

Pipe a tube 20 shell border around base. Drop tube 2 stringwork from top edge and pipe a tube 20 shell border around the top. To make roses, first pipe tube 3 stems across latticework, working carefully. Next make roses on a flower nail and lift off with a scissors, placing them carefully on stems to create a spray arrangement. Make roses and buds with tube 104. To make leaves, fill bag with icing, flatten tip and cut into arrow shape. Cut a tiny slit in point of arrow for center rib. Provides 50 wedding-size servings or 20 party-size servings.

GARDEN WEDDING CAKE
shown on opposite page

In advance, make a total of at least fifty cosmos, marigolds, nasturtiums and zinnias, attaching some to wire stems. Directions for making cosmos and zinnias start on page 90.

Next bake and ice the following tiers: 14" x 4" and 6" x 3" round and 10" x 4" square. Assemble with 8" round separator plates and 5" Grecian pillars.

To decorate, pipe tube 19 shell border around top and base of 14" tier. Drape tube 21 "e" motion garland around side of this tier and pipe tube 17 fleur-de-lis at points where garlands meet. Drop three rows of tube 2 string over each garland, and finish with a tiny knot. On top of 10" tier, pipe tube 16 scallops around separator plate. Pipe tube 16 shell border around base and top of this tier, tube 21 garlands and tube 17 fleur-de-lis. Top garlands with tube 2 stringwork and knot.

On top tier, pipe tube 16 shell border around top and base, relaxing pressure used on second tier. Drape tube 17 garlands around side, add tube 17 fleur-de-lis and tube 2 string. Place petite Bridal Couple on 3¼" Heart Base on top of tier and surround with flowers. Place additional flowers on each tier. Invert 2" plastic Lace Bell on a mound of icing on lower separator plate and arrange flowers in "vase". Serves 158.

RETURN OF AN OLD TRADITION

A cake for the groom

LONG AGO, in England*, the custom of having two cakes at a wedding celebration originated. Before this time, the bride's cake was usually a platter of small cakes, purposely small so that boisterous guests could pelt them at the bride and groom as they entered the door of their new home. Hopeful maidens saved some of the little cakes to "sleep on" and induce pleasant dreams of a suitor. By the end of the 18th century, French patissiers had transformed the humble little confections into towering works of art, similar to today's wedding cakes. That is when the resourceful British, to save the beautiful bridal cake from destruction, began to serve a second cake—for "breaking and throwing" . . . and later, in more refined times, for cutting and taking home.

Groom's cakes are again becoming popular at today's receptions. Usually slices

*The Wilton Book of Wedding Cakes

Overture

A cake with a promise of
happy years ahead.
Stately arches frame a
replica-cake for the
first anniversary.

Allegro

Delicate beauty in a bridal cake
trimmed with lattice and sunny flowers

Decorating directions for both cakes start on page 69

Azalea

. . . romantic simplicity
in a rosy cake
accented with a
fresh bouquet

Decorating directions start on page 68

56

Cake decorated by Valarie Wozney

CONGRATULATIONS! YOU WON!

We asked our readers to dream up cakes for "the favorite men in their lives" and the response was terrific. It wasn't easy to choose three winners, so we wound up with three Honorable Mention awards in addition to the three top prizes.

THREE HAPPY GREETINGS

First prize, a $25 Gift Certificate, was won by **Kathy Weinstein** of Fremont, California, for a delightful cake she baked for her husband's birthday. It's topped by three pandas baked in chocolate molds, and three heart cupcakes with the names of their children. Base is 12″ x 18″.

A BIG ONE GOT AWAY

Second prize of a $15 Gift Certificate was earned by **Carol Roberts** of Richland, Wisconsin for her "fisherman's cake."

A 9″ x 13″ sheet cake, thickly swirled with icing "waves" was the base for a boat baked in the Egg-shaped pan. Carol molded her fish in chocolate, but we used summer coating for this reproduction. A Tangled Fisherman figure sits sadly in the boat.

DOWN THE SLOPES

A cleverly-designed "snowmobile cake" won the $15 Gift Certificate and third prize for **Sandra Chaffer** of Columbiaville, Mich.

Sandra made her S-curve snowmobile track from a cake baked in a Horseshoe Pan, cut in half with the halves positioned to form curves. Her cake was swirled with fluffy marshmallow icing and accented with piped evergreen trees and candles. She pulled a tablespoon down the curve to create a trail for two Snowmobiles.

HONORABLE MENTIONS

Another fisherman's cake won a $5 Gift Certificate for **Mrs. Robert Estes** of Springfield, Virginia. She baked cakes in round mini-tier pans, cut and stacked the two smaller tiers to make the bank, and used the largest for a "pond". Flowers, vines, leaves and mushrooms piped around the edges of the pond gave it a natural look. Mrs. Estes added a frog, duck and water lilies. The tangled Fisherman, taken off his stand, sits on the bank.

Shirley Brooke of Schwenksville, Pennsylvania, received Honorable Mention and a $5 Gift Certificate for her motorcycle cake. She made the motorcycle of royal icing piped on both sides of cardboard, then propped it with toothpicks on a cake decorated to look like a park.

A $5 Gift Certificate also goes to **Barbara Foote** of Springfield, Massachusetts for her unique tractor cake. She carved the tractor from a loaf size pound cake, added seat and steering wheel made of gum paste, piped other details in icing. Cookies with wafer candy "hub caps" made the wheels. Barbara set her realistic tractor on a chocolate-iced sheet cake.

Mother

CROWN HER DAY WITH AN EXQUISITE CAKE

QUEEN OF HEARTS, a cake to make mom queen for her day. To decorate, tape crown and heart patterns to Cake-Side Formers, cover with wax paper and pipe patterns with tube 2 and Color Flow icing, filling in jewel areas. Make 1 heart and 6 crown sections. Dry thoroughly, then fill in jewels with tinted piping gel.

Next pipe a dozen tube 103 roses and a dozen buds. Also pipe tube 65 leaves. Attach flowers and leaves to wires and assemble into 2 sprays and 2 petite bouquets. Ice a 10" x 4" cake and a 6" x 1" styrofoam (or cake) circle. Position circle toward rear of 10" cake. Now carefully peel crown sections and heart off wax paper. Attach heart with icing. Set crown sections around circle and secure with icing.

Pipe base border with tube 10 beading, cake top and sides with tube 2

beading and position flowers. Spectacular, and surprisingly quick to do. Serves 14.

PORTRAIT tells Mother how much her children love her. To make the Color Flow children's silhouettes, use our boy-girl patterns or sketch your own. The six-sided cake has room for six portraits, but for fewer children, trim sides with lacy fans.

Make tube 104 full and half carnations. Pipe tube 1 lettering on Miniature Easel.

Now bake and ice a 12" x 4" hexagon cake. Pipe tube 19 rosette border around base. Outline side sections of cake with tube 16 stars.

To make rosette fans, mark curves on top and sides of cake with toothpick. Do side panels first. (To make decorating easier, elevate the cake slightly on one

Continued on page 70

Americana: THE 1898 OLDSMOBILE

THE EARLY DAYS of the automobile were exciting times, as daring drivers got up to such hair-raising speeds as 15 miles per hour. Modern antique and classic car buffs get just as much fun restoring and polishing their treasured cars, and displaying them at rallies and auctions. Any antique-car fancier or model-car maker can enjoy this classic car cake, graced by a historic Oldsmobile.

DECORATE THE CAKE

First prepare Oldsmobile background plaque, logo and car sections, using patterns and Color Flow technique. Outline in tube 2, fill in and dry thoroughly. Pipe tube 1 trim on car sections and beading on logo and plaque.

Next, bake and ice a 10" x 4" square cake and ice white. Pipe tube 364 shell border around bottom and tube 362 border around top of cake. Overpipe bottom border with tube 3 swirls in darker blue. To assemble car: place plaque on top of cake, supporting it on five oblong sugar cubes—one in the middle and one under each corner. Position two back tires and driver as per pattern. Next, add body of car, then secure fenders in place. Next, add two front tires, and the yellow headlight. Finally, attach logo to side of cake.

60

Americana: THE FLYING CLOUD

The Flying Cloud, built by David McKay and launched in 1851, is probably the most famous of the clippers. Not the earliest or the largest, the Flying Cloud was most consistently fast under all circumstances, and in all weathers. She set a record sailing from New York to California, making the trip around the Horn in 89 days. Now this great clipper adorns a cake to delight sailing buffs of any age.

DECORATE THE CAKE

First, tape ship patterns to cardboards and cover with wax paper or clear plastic wrap; outline each with tube 2, and flow in colors. Rigging is added when cake is assembled. Make panel for top of cake, outline and flow in white Color Flow icing, and while it is still wet, brush in pastel blue and beige and swirl lightly to give cloud effect to sky. Dry all thoroughly.

Bake and ice a 9" x 13" x 4" cake. Place on foil covered board and pipe tube 22 shell borders around top and base of cake, and tube 22 scrolls at each corner. Pipe tube 2 lettering on side. Position panel on top of cake on nine oblong sugar cubes (3 on each side and 3 in the middle). Pipe tube 16 rope border around plaque.

To assemble ship, follow A, B, C sequence of patterns: first position the two-mast section at far right side; second, the single mast with four sails; third, single sail and pennant; fourth, the three small sails at far left; and fifth, the body of the ship. Pipe tube 1 rigging on each layer as you add it, allowing at least ten minutes for it to dry. Finally, use spatula to make waves of blue-green icing, with some white touches.

The Dainty Australian Method of decorating

BY MICHAEL NITZSCHE

HOW THE EXPERTS DO IT

While Australian cake decorating is strongly influenced by the English method, it is nevertheless so individual that the two could never be confused. The Australians have departed from the formal geometrical designs of the English for cakes that are softly shaped and touched with the most delicate of icing lace and stringwork. Here, Michael Nitzsche presents first a true Australian design cake and then an attractive American adaptation of the lovely Australian "look".

HIGHLIGHTS OF THE STYLE

Australian cakes can be identified instantly by the unique way in which they are covered. Both English and Australian festive cakes are usually fruitcake, first covered on top and sides with rolled almond paste to produce a smooth, perfectly level surface.

But rather than covering the almond

paste with a smoothly applied coat of icing as the English do, the Australian decorators prefer to top their almond paste cover with a second one-piece cover of satiny rolled fondant. This gives the cake a seamless and soft-contoured effect no coat of icing could possibly achieve.

One of the prettiest features of Australian decorating is the marvelous variety of icing lace, net and embroidery. Breathtaking Australian "extension work" (a 3-dimensional stringwork) adds the frilly look of fringe or sheer, pleated ruffles.

Australian decorators prefer to trim their cakes with flowers hand-shaped of gum paste, wonderfully realistic looking. However, they also use flowers piped of icing just as we do.

The complete story of Australian decorating will be told in the second volume of "The Wilton Way of Cake Decorating", now in preparation.

PREPARING THE CAKE

Cover an 8" x 3" round fruitcake with almond paste as directed on page 94. Brush with egg white or apricot glaze.

Next, make rolled fondant, page 94. Tint pale pink, then knead until smooth and pliable. Sprinkle board with cornstarch and roll out to cover cake. Lift onto cake with rolling pin, then dust hands with cornstarch and gently smooth and fit icing to cake with palms. Cut excess icing from base and the cake is ready to decorate.

MODELLING THE ROSES

First make a recipe of gum paste, page 32. Divide and tint pale and deep pink. First roll a marble-size piece of deep pink paste between thumb and fingers into a flat petal shape with sharp top edge. Roll in spiral for tight center bud. Build a base for bud with more paste. Next, shape small and large petals in lighter pink. Beginning with smallest petals, dampen and press onto base of bud, one at a time. Overlap and curve petals outward as you go around. Do 4 rows in all. For rosebud, roll a center bud and spiral a single large petal around it. For stem, wrap green florist tape around lengths of florist wire, binding marzipan leaves on to end of one wire, pushing another into base of rosebud. Fashion a green gum paste calyx for rosebud.

DECORATING THE CAKE

First measure cake. Take a strip of greaseproof paper 1¾" wide and long enough to reach around cake. Fold into 12ths. Cut ½" deep scallops into top and bottom, unfold, pin to cake sides ½" above base. Mark with toothpick, remove. Edge base with tube 15 shells. Pipe free hand embroidery with tube 1. Begin extension work.

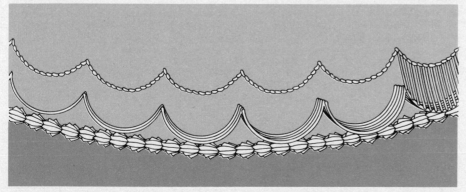

EXTENSION WORK

1. Pipe extension work. Outline bottom curves of pattern with lines of icing using tube 1 and royal icing. Then overpipe 4 times, letting each line of icing dry before piping another atop it. Position each line along outer edge of line beneath it to give the extension work an outward slant.

2. Brush to smooth. Go over completed extension work with moist art brush and thinned icing.

3. Pipe strings. Use tube 000, and follow pattern that has been "picked" into fondant. Beginning at top scallop, touch icing to cake, pull out slightly and let drop. Touch back at edge of extension work and break off pressure. To keep lines straight, do those at points of scallop first, then one directly in center. Divide space on either side and keep dividing open spaces until scallop is covered with string. Repeat around cake.

4. Add beads, loops. Then pipe beading over marks of upper scallops, and tiny scalloped edging with tube 1. Cover rough ends of string at edge of extension work with beads and drape little half-inch loops beneath them, using tube 1. (4 to a scallop.)

Position rose spray at top, using a bit of icing to secure it. Your lovely Australian cake is complete! Serves 12.

Directions for making the look-alike "Wedding Bell" cake above, using quick American techniques, are on page 70.

SHOW DAD he's first in the hearts of the family. Bake him a cake that's trimmed with a fanciful coat of arms and a bold, good-looking border.

The coat of arms is done in three sections for dimensional effect. First the red section with the scrolled edges, then the brown shield, and last the two pieces that sit on top of the shield. Crown, heart, letters and fleur-de-lis are done separately, too. Make all the pieces in advance, using CELEBRATE! II pattern and Color Flow technique. When thoroughly dry, assemble with dots of icing.

Just before Father's Day, bake a two-layer 10″ square cake, fill and ice. Use his favorite flavors for this. Pipe a tube 21 reverse shell border at base. Measure and mark top edge of cake for border, a fleur-de-lis variation. Using tube 20, pipe large shell on top of cake, at marks, flanked by two curving shells. Pipe two "C" shaped scrolls below on sides of cake. Add stars where curves meet, and between fleur-de-lis on top edge of cake.

Set coat of arms in center of cake on flat sugar cubes, or on mounds of icing. Serves 20, delights Dad!

WILD ROSES FOR MOM on a petal-shaped cake that's sweet as she is! So simple to make, because you can pipe the pretty flowers long before Mother's Day.

Use tube 102 for petals, tube 1 for tiny yellow dot stamens. "Paint" eight 2½″ plastic filigree scrolls with thinned yellow icing at the same time and reserve.

Then on Mom's big day, all you need do is bake a two-layer cake in a pair of 9″ petal-shaped pans. Ice cake same pale yellow as filigree and border with neat white shells, using tube 21 at bottom and tube 19 at top. Pipe big mound of icing on cake top and tiny mounds on each curve of sides, then position reserved wild roses in a "bouquet" at top and clusters at sides. Add tube 65 leaves. Press in filigree, securing with icing, and write a loving message with tube 2 on top. Watch Mom go wild over it! Serves 8 hearty dessert lovers or 16 "tea party" guests.

A ROYAL CAKE FOR FATHER

Quick & Pretty

A FLOWERY CAKE FOR MOM

64

Presidential Portrait Cakes

SIX OF OUR best-loved presidents are honored in these striking cakes. Each cake is a showpiece in its own right, and the six grouped together make an impressive bicentennial display.

Each cake bears the name of the president and the dates he held office, and each is trimmed with his state flower.

Construction is similar for all. The flowers and portraits can be prepared well in advance, and then the cakes put together rather quickly.

HOW TO MAKE THE PORTRAITS

All the portraits are made using the same technique—very much like "painting with numbers". Tube 13, with a light pressure, is used for all, except for very tiny areas, such as around the eyes, which are filled in with tube 1. Each area of the CELEBRATE! II patterns has a number which corresponds with a tint of icing.

These are the colors we used:

1. A light flesh tint
2. Golden beige
3. A deeper, reddish beige
4. A medium rust color
5. Light grey
6. Deep grey
7. Dark brown
8. Light brown
9. Light blue
10. Medium blue
11. Deep blue-grey
12. Light crimson-red
13. Crimson
14. Gold color
15. Cream white
16. Reddish-brown

Numbers 1 through 4, with occasional use of number 7, are used for all the skin tones. Numbers 5, 6, 10 and 11 are used for the eyes. Number 15 is also used for the eyes, and for the white hair of Washington and Jefferson.

Start by taping the pattern to a smooth surface and taping wax paper smoothly over it. Tint royal icing in colors 1-4, 5, 6, 7, 10, 11 and 15. Fit 10 paper decorating cones with tube 13 and fill with the above colors of icing. Mark each bag with the color number and cover tips of tubes with a damp cloth so they are ready for use.

Now, starting at the top of the face, fill the pattern areas with tiny stars. Do not attempt to do all areas of one color at once, but work from top to bottom, changing colors as the pattern areas indicate.

When the face is finished, do the hair area, then the suit and shirt. Add the background using colors 9, 10, 12 and 13.

FINALLY, add frames to the portraits. For Washington, edge portrait with tube 45, wide end toward the picture. Trim with tube 65 leaves, and tube 1 scrolls.

For Lincoln, edge portrait with tube 15 rope border, adding fleur-de-lis with the same tube at top.

For Jefferson, frame with a tube 8 ball border. Roosevelt's portrait is edged with tube 17 stars. For Eisenhower, frame with tube 6, trim with tube 2. Finish the Kennedy portrait with a tube 8 ball frame.

WHEN PORTRAIT IS DRY, carefully peel off the wax paper, turn over and cover the back with softened Color Flow icing, using a cut bag. Cover the frame area with matching icing and use white icing for the rest. This will add strength to the portrait. On all of the portraits, except those of Eisenhower and Kennedy, lay two popsicle sticks, with ends protruding from the base of the portrait, on the back. Then proceed to flow in the back of the portrait. The sticks will make it easier to prop the portrait on the base cake. Dry very thoroughly. Your portrait is ready to set on the cake!

HOW TO DECORATE THE BOOK CAKES

All the book cakes are decorated the same. Bake cakes in book pans and position on board the same size. Ice top as smoothly as possible. Ice sides in contrasting color and mark pages with the lines of a fork. Pipe a tube 80 strip all around the base of the cake to simulate binding. Add lettering with tube 2.

When assembling the book cakes on base cakes, prop them on a piece of iced styrofoam to give height at the back. Set several ¼" dowels into the base cake to support the weight of the book.

Bookmarks are ribbon.

GEORGE WASHINGTON

Make a quantity of American Beauty roses and buds, using tube 104. Put some of the flowers on florist wire stems.

For base, bake two cakes, a 12" x 4" round and a 9" x 13" sheet cake, 2" high. Cut the sheet cake into 2 layers, each 4½" x 12". Fill and stack. Cut the 12" round cake in half and place halves on either side to form a 16½" long oval. Ice and place on foil-covered board, double in thickness.

To decorate: pipe tube 32 white shell border around base of oval cake, and tube 18 shell border around top. Pipe tube 3 scrollwork to frame name and dates, and do lettering with tube 2. Place book on top of cake and add ribbon bookmark. Position portrait and roses and pipe tube 67 leaves. Serves 40.

ABRAHAM LINCOLN

Make violets with tube 59 and tube 67 leaves. Mount flowers and leaves on florist wire with icing.

Now, bake a 12" x 4" square cake and ice white. Place on gold foil-covered board. Pipe tube 17 shell border around base of cake. About 1½" from each corner of cake, mark a scroll shape. Then pipe tube 2 lattice between marks and corner. Frame lattice with tube 17, using an "e" motion.

Pipe tube 16 shell border around top edge of cake and down edge of cake at each corner. Pipe tube 2 lettering and dates.

To complete, position book cake and portrait. Arrange flowers and leaves across back of cake and place cluster of flowers at one corner. Serves 42.

THOMAS JEFFERSON

Make dogwood blossoms in advance, following directions on page 90.

Bake and ice a 12" x 18" x 4" cake. Place on foil covered board. Pipe tube 16 shell border on top edge of cake. Pipe a tube 199 pillar at each corner of the cake, and 2 pillars on either side of it, starting at bottom with heavy pressure, and drawing tube up to the top of the cake with even pressure. Pipe tube 16 "e" motion frame around top and base of each pillar. Finish base of cake with a tube 18 garland border. Pipe name and dates with tube 2. Place portrait and book cake. Pipe mounds of icing at corners of cake and in front of portrait, and add flowers. Pipe tube 65 leaves. Serves 44.

FRANKLIN DELANO ROOSEVELT

Prepare roses and rosebuds, and mount some on florist wire.

Next, bake and ice a 12" x 18" x 4" cake. Place on foil covered board. Pipe tube 19 star border around base and top of cake. Then pipe a row of tube 19 stars down the side of the cake at each corner and frame these with graduated rows of tube 19 stars; seven, five, three, two and one. Pipe tube 2 lettering and dates. Position book cake and portrait, add roses and buds. Trim with tube 65 leaves. Serves 44.

DWIGHT D. EISENHOWER

First make sunflowers following directions on page 90. Pipe tube 70 leaves. Dry, and mount some of the leaves and flowers on florist wire.

Bake and ice a 12"x4" square cake. Place on a foil covered board. Pipe tube 21 reverse shell border around base and top of cake. Pipe tube 2 lettering and a semicircle of blue tube 14 stars below the name and dates. Position book cake. Set portrait at front of cake, attaching with icing. Arrange flowers and leaves. Serves 42.

JOHN FITZGERALD KENNEDY

Make mayflowers as directed on page 90.

Bake and ice a 9"x13"x4" cake and place on a foil covered board. Pipe tube 32 shell border around base of cake and trim each shell with a tube 3 scroll. Pipe tube 2 lettering and dates. Position book cake. Place portrait at front of cake and attach with icing. Pipe tube 67 leaves and arrange flowers on top of them. Serves 27.

THE THREE WISE MEN
Shown on page 9

Decorate these beautiful stylized versions for a Christmas or Twelfth Night party.

Bake two cakes in Long Loaf Pans and cut in half to make four 8" x 4" cakes. Three halves make the three wise men, and the other half is cut into 4" x 2" rectangles to make the gifts. For crowns, bake 3 cakes in small Wonder Molds. Ice one loaf cake yellow, one pink, one green, and ice gifts to match.

These cakes are meant to be decorated in an imaginative, creative manner—so tint some icing, get out the patterns and have fun! We used tube 2 for straight lines, dots, scallops and cornelli. Faces were filled in with tube 18 stars; tube 22 stars filled in sides, backs, and two of the crowns. Most of the decorating on the gifts was done with tube 2. Serves 27.

AN AMERICAN COUSIN
shown on page 42

A beautiful cake. Inspired by the English-Nirvana method, but executed in the free American style.

First, prepare top plaque and twelve beveled sections for the base, using CELE-BRATE! II patterns and Color Flow technique. When dry, edge plaque with tube 2 beading and trim with beading and scrolls. Use same tube to trim bevels with scrolls.

Also in advance, make a quantity of tube 102 wild roses with tube 1 stamens. Pipe tube 65 leaves. Mount leaves and some of the flowers on florist wire.

Next, bake a 9" 2-layer hexagon cake and ice. Place on foil-covered board 3" larger. To support top plaque pipe 6 triangles of icing lines on the cake top, using tube 4. Overpipe these twice to provide final elevation of about one-quarter inch.

Now attach the bevel panels around base. First pipe a tube 8 line of icing at base of cake, extending about 1" in each direction from angle of cake. Set a bevel section in position and add second bevel so that two bevels line up exactly at angle of cake. Continue to place bevel sections at each angle of cake, taking care to keep tops of bevels at same height. Pipe tube 2 beading around the bevels. Attach flowers to sides of cake just above bevels. Trim with tube 65 leaves. Pipe dots of icing on riser lines on top of cake and carefully set top plaque in position.

Pipe mound of icing in center opening. Arrange flowers and leaves. Serves 12.

A SALUTE TO AMERICAN DECORATORS
Shown on page 10

First make chef figures from marzipan. (Directions are on page 96.) Make drop flowers with tube 217 and mount a few on wires. Next, bake 3 round tiers, 14" x 4", 10" x 4" and 6" x 3". Ice in different pastel colors to contrast with chef's white outfits. Assemble tiers, using 12" separator plates and 5" Grecian Pillars. Place on gold foil-covered board.

Pipe a shell border around bottom of each tier; tube 508 on lowest tier, tube 506 on middle tier and tube 504 on top tier, all partially finished.

Pipe tube 21 puff border around top of 12" and 10" tiers, and drape each puff with tube 3 stringwork. Leave each border incomplete to indicate work in progress. On top tier, pipe tube 19 puffs around top, with tube 3 stringwork.

Make two banners from colored paper and long pins. Add lettering with tube 1 and insert the banners in two chefs' hands.

Now position chefs on cake, anchoring with icing and toothpicks. One of the chefs on the top tier stands on a small Heart Ornament Base. The chef on the bottom tier is on a Mini-Bench, iced and trimmed with tube 13 shells. Add drop flowers. Yields 48 party-sized portions.

HAPPY SPRING
shown on page 28

As refreshing as a sunny spring day, this happy cake is trimmed with pussy willows and golden daffodils.

First make daffodils; pipe five curved petals with tube 104 and yellow icing. Pinch tips of petals for life-like look. Then build up darker yellow center cup, working in a spiral with tube 3. Edge with tube 1 dots. Pull out stamen with tube 0. Let dry.

Next bake a 2-layer 9" x 13" cake and ice with buttercream. Pipe tube 6 bulb border around bottom of cake and scrolls on sides. Pipe message with tube 1.

For oval frame, cut template about 10" x 7½". Lay it on top of cake and trace with toothpick. Outline oval with tube 4. Then pipe tube 4 shells on each side of this outline, with shells facing the same direction. Pipe another row of tube 4 shells on top of the oval outline, with its shells facing opposite direction. Now darken the icing a little and using tube 13 pipe a shell border on both sides of this top row of shells, facing same direction as the first two rows. Inside the oval, pipe tube 2 scallops.

Pipe pussy willows right on the cake, following directions on page 90. Pipe tube 3 stems for daffodils and long leaves with tube 67. Attach flowers with icing. Finish with tube 46 ribbon bow. Trim side of cake with more pussy willows and a daffodil. Serves 24.

HEARTS AND ROSES
Shown on page 17

pipe a garland of tube 21 puffs around bottom. Outline puffs with tube 14 zigzags. Place tube 101s roses between every second puff and pipe tube 67 leaves. With tube 16, make scallop design around top and sides of cake. Overpipe with an "e" motion for fluffy effect. Fill in area between the two sets of scallops with tube 2 dots.

Carefully position lattice hearts atop cake and add cluster of rosebuds and wired leaves in center openings. Pipe mound of icing as base for larger roses and leaves. Serves 12 to 15.

QUICK AND PRETTY CAKES (continued)
shown on pages 40 and 41

strip, add tube 65 leaves. Set Babe in Bower on top of cake and trim with flowers and add tube 65 leaves. Serves 14, looks like a work of art.

TELL THE GOOD NEWS at a gala engagement party. The pretty cake will be the center of attention.

In advance, make tube 224 pink drop flowers. Bake and ice two cookies for "him" and "her", using Really Big hand cutter. Decorate hands with tube 104 cuff for man, ruffles for both, and tube 3 beading on the lady's. Pipe tube 7 hearts on backs of both hands. Pipe tube 3 pink nails for the lady and brush to make nail shapes. Pipe a tube 4 zigzag ring with a tube 3 "stone" circled by tube 1 dots.

Tape wax paper over lattice patterns and pipe with tube 1. Pipe outside edges with tube 3. Set aside and dry.

Now bake and ice 9"x13" two-layer cake. Affix lattice work to cake with dots of icing. Pipe tube 16 borders around curved edges of lattice. Arrange hands on top of cake and pipe tube 1 lettering. Border cake with tube 18 shells at base, tube 16 shells at top. Pipe mounds of icing at corners of cake and position flowers. Then pipe small icing garland between latticework and attach more flowers. Trim flowers with tube 65 leaves. Serves 24.

CROCHET A CAKE! Pipe the popular Granny Square motif in pretty pastels, or colors taken from your favorite sweater or afghan.

Bake and ice an 8"x3" square cake. With a toothpick, mark top of cake into grid, using CELEBRATE! II pattern. Start in center and pipe cross-shaped motif. Each "arm" of cross is piped with three touching tube 18 shells. Move out one row, change color, and pipe eight triple shells around cross. Continue until you reach the edge. The picture will be your guide. Pipe cross motifs on sides of cake and accent with tube 4 dots. Finish with tube 21 shell border. Serves 12 at a crochet session in your home.

HOW TO MAKE
THE BASKET CAKES
Shown on pages 24 and 25

STRAWBERRY BASKET

Bake a 5″ x 3″ square cake, chill and then taper with sharp knife to basket shape. Prepare marzipan (recipe, page 96). Roll and cut strips of untinted marzipan to make sides of basket, and attach to cake with royal icing. Tint marzipan to make strawberries and roll in red crystal sugar. Make leaves of green tinted marzipan, tracing veins with back of knife. Dry some leaves on a curved form. Pipe tube 103 strawberry blossoms, add centers with tube 3 and let dry.

Now bake an 8″ x 4″ square cake (2 layers) and ice with buttercream. Pipe a tube 22 puff border around base of cake, and a tube 22 double shell border around top. Now place basket cake on top and pipe a mound of icing to anchor berries. Arrange strawberries, blossoms and leaves in and around basket and place some at base of cake. Serves 12.

CHERRY BASKET

First make cherries and leaves from tinted marzipan and mount cherries on short stems of florist wire. (See marzipan recipe on page 96.) When dry, brush cherries with glaze made with ½ cup corn syrup heated with 2 tablespoons water.

Bake a 5″ round cake 4″ high and taper with a knife to basket shape. To make basket weave covering: fit one decorating bag with tube 3 and fill with gold icing, fit another with tube 2 and fill with yellow icing. Pipe two vertical lines of icing with first bag, then with second bag pipe horizontal rows about ½″ long across vertical line. Begin at top and leave about ¼″ between each one as you move downward. Pipe second vertical lines where horizontal lines end, and repeat, placing second row of horizontal lines between first row.

Pipe a tube 6 bulb border of gold icing around base of basket. At top of basket, using light pressure, drop a row of overlapping tube 6 strings below the rim. Next, pipe a double row of tube 6 bulbs, again using light pressure.

Cut strip of cardboard (about as stiff as back of tablet) one or two inches wide and about 13 inches long. Attach wax paper to one side. Next, set 6″ round pan bottom side up. Attach cardboard to sides of pan so it makes an arch (or handle) above it that is 6 inches wide at base and 5 inches high from bottom of pan to top of arch, wax paper outside. Now use tube 6 with

gold icing and pipe 3 lines side by side over full length of arch. Pipe 2 more on top of 3, then 1 on top of 2 to make triangle. "Bind" handle with crisscross tube 2 lines in yellow. When dry, peel off paper. After basket is filled with marzipan cherries and leaves, attach handle with royal icing and let dry thoroughly. Trim with ribbon bow. Serves 8.

FLOWER BASKET

In advance, make drop flowers in bright colors with tubes 190, 194, 2E, 2D, 1B, 1C and 1F. Make tube 112 leaves and let dry; mount flowers and leaves on florist wire. (See page 90.)

Bake an 8″ x 4″ round cake, two layers, and ice. Place on serving tray. Next comes basket weave. Fit two decorating bags, filled with green icing, with tubes 5 and 48. Pipe a vertical line of icing with tube 5. Then, with second bag, pipe horizontal bands of ribbed icing about ½″ long across vertical line, beginning at top and leaving about ⅜″ space between each as you move downward. Repeat to cover sides of cake. Pipe tube 19 rope border at top and bottom of cake and tube 19 rope handles.

Stick wired flowers into cake top to create bouquet, adding wired leaves for accent. Place ribbon bow on one handle, and set posy of wired flowers tied with matching ribbon beside cake. Serves 10.

FABULOUS EASTER EGGS
shown on page 27

These delicate, fanciful Easter treasures are jewels of the decorator's art. Carefully stored they may be brought out for many springs to come to enhance the Easter celebration.

Use an egg white sugar mixture to mold all the eggs in plastic Egg Molds. Dry until firm crust forms, then carefully scoop out the damp sugar leaving a shell about 1/16″ to ¼″ thick. Dry again for at least five hours before decorating. Royal icing is used for all trims.

BASKET EGG. Pipe violets with tube 59°, leaves with tube 67, dry and mount on florist wire. Mold egg in 3″ mold. Drop out on cardboard and use thread to cut off narrow end to form basket shape. Finish egg as described above.

Trace open side of 5″ egg, tape to board

and tape wax paper over. This is pattern for handle. Using tube 4, trace pattern, then pipe another line just inside of first. Overpipe twice, then fill in with tube 1 beading. Dry.

Base is made from an ice cream cone, with point cut off with a sharp knife. Cut two indentations on either side of base to hold handle. Trim base with tube 4 beading at bottom and top, tube 1 string. Put two halves of sugar basket together with icing and trim with tube 1 scrolls and beading. Dry. Prop with crumpled foil, pipe mound of icing inside, and arrange flowers and leaves.

Set handle in indentations on base, fix with icing. Finish with a ribbon drape.

SWAN EGG. Mold egg in 3″ egg mold. After dropping out on cardboard, cut one half-egg shape in two with a thread to form doors. Trace open end of 3″ egg mold, tape on board and tape wax paper over. Figure pipe swan on this wax paper with tube 6, using picture as guide. Trim inside of "doors" with tube 1 scallops, tube 2 leaf design. Trim inside of whole half-egg with tube 1 scallops.

All parts of this egg are assembled with airplane glue. To make base, glue two large flat sugar cubes together, side by

side. Then glue two smaller cube-shaped cubes on top of them, matching seams. Trim corners of cubes with sharp knife to make oval shape. Ice and pipe tube 4 trim. Assemble egg on base, propping carefully until thoroughly dry, about 48 hours. Glue swan and scrolls in place, dry again.

EGG IN TREE. Mold egg in 4¼″ mold. While damp, cut opening in one half-egg with thread.

Make tree by twisting three 9″ lengths of heavy florist wire together for main trunk. Bind ends of wire into loops for widespread base. Form three main branches from twelve fine wires twisted together. Wire to trunk. Shape branches into position to hold egg, using plastic mold as form. Pipe wires with tube 21 to form "bark" effect. Pipe finer branches at ends with tube 2.

Trace open side of 4½″ egg mold and draw pattern for branches inside molded egg within this shape. Tape wax paper over and pipe branches with tube 2. Figure pipe bluebirds on wax paper with tube 4.

Place inner branches inside whole half-egg, attach with icing. Pipe tube 65s leaves. Add bird with dots of icing. Put two halves of egg together with icing and trim egg with tube 1. Dry. Place egg in tree, attach second bird.

A Bridal Bouquet

HEART ENGAGEMENT CAKE
Shown on page 18

Make tube 102 apple blossoms and rose-buds and tube 101s miniature apple blossoms in advance, and set aside to dry.

Bake and ice a 9″ x 4″ heart cake. Pipe pillar border around cake. For pillars, press out a tube 199 standing shell directly on board at base of cake. Let build up slightly so bottom of shell will flatten out. Keeping an even pressure, pull upward so shell flows into pillar shape. Cut off at cake edge. Pipe pillars all around cake, 1″ apart at base. Pipe tube 20 frame with "e" motion around base of pillars.

Drop a pink tube 2 guideline to connect each pillar at top and go over it with a white tube 14 drape. Between bases of pillars pipe large hearts with tube 9; pipe smaller hearts at the tops of pillars with tube 8. (Make hearts by applying pressure with tube held at a 45° angle. Relax pressure as you move to a perpendicular position. Move away to form point.)

Do tube 2 lettering and make scalloped border around top with tube 14 scrollwork. Make a garland of the flowers and add tube 66 leaves, tube 1 stems. Position dove at each end of garland and pipe a tube 1 ribbon leading to each dove. Serves 12.

HEART WEDDING CAKE
Shown on page 19

In advance, make many tube 102 and 103 roses and apple blossoms and tube 101s apple blossoms. Also make drop flowers using tube 106. When dry, mount some flowers on wire to make bouquet. Make tube 7 hearts ahead of time and dry. (Directions for hearts and pillars, above.)

Bake 14″ x 4″ and 10″ x 4″ and 6″ x 3″ round tiers. Ice 14″ tier pink and others white. Assemble with 5″ Grecian pillars.

Pipe tube 199 pillars around the sides of lower tier. Pipe a tube 21 puff border edged by a tube 16 zigzag border around base of each tier. Drop 2 rows of tube 4 stringwork in deep pink from tops of pillars and cover each row with a tube 14 c-motion drape. Now pipe a tube 21 shell border around top edge of 14″ tier. Attach

one deep pink heart between each pillar with dot of icing, and a white heart at top of each pillar. Next, pipe a tube 17 shell border around top edge of 10″ tier and tube 16 zigzag around the separator plate. Pipe tube 16 shells around top of 6″ tier. Arrange garlands of flowers around 10″ tier. Trim with tube 65 leaves. Attach pale pink double hearts around sides of top tier with icing, and secure 2 small doves with icing. Drape a tube 1 ribbon of deep pink stringwork between doves. Top the cake with a bouquet of wired flowers. Position figures within pillars, add a spray of flowers and tube 65 leaves. Serves 155.

BUTTERFLY ENGAGEMENT CAKE
shown on page 46

Bright butterflies flutter above blossoms on a cake that forecasts the bridal cake.

Make butterfly wings with Color Flow method and CELEBRATE! II patterns. To assemble, pipe a thick line of icing on wax paper for body. Double a fine wire and bend ends out for antenna. Lay wire in icing. Immediately push wings into icing and prop with cotton. (There will be a "tail" of wire extending from bottom of body. This will be inserted into cake.) Dry thoroughly. Make tube 190 and 124 drop flowers with tube 2 centers. Dry.

Now, bake and ice a 10″ x 4″ square cake. Mark curves on either side of cake corners. Pipe diagonal lines of tube 3 stringwork from one mark to next so they wrap around the corner. Then pipe another series of diagonal lines with tube 3 to create crisscross lattice. Pipe scrolls at edges of lattice with tube 5. Add a tube 3 heart at each corner. Pipe a tube 5 bulb border around base and top of cake.

Now pipe mound of icing in center of cake and arrange flowers over it. Trim with tube 65 leaves. Position wired butterflies. Serves 20.

BUTTERFLY WEDDING CAKE
Shown on page 47.

First prepare filigree butterflies. Tape pattern on cardboard and tape wax paper smoothly over it. Outline with royal icing thinned with egg white, using tube 2. Overpipe for extra strength. When dry, peel off wax paper and overpipe back. Pipe thick line of icing on wax paper, set two wings in position and prop while drying. Make extras, they're extremely fragile.

Make tube 190 and 225 drop flowers.

Now bake, ice and assemble 14″ x 4″, 12″ x 4″ and 8″ x 3″ square tiers. Use 3″ filigree pillars and 9″ square separator plates. Pipe tube 6 bulb borders around base of each tier, and tube 4 bulb borders around top of each tier. Pipe tube 4 latticework at corners of 8″ and 12″ tiers. Pipe tube 6 scrolls to frame corners of each tier.

Pipe mounds of icing at corners of two lower tiers and press in drop flowers. Attach butterflies with icing, handling carefully. Place one large butterfly on Decorator Base on top of cake. Serves 200.

CRYSTAL
Shown on page 48

In advance make tube 104 roses and buds. Next bake 18″x4″ and 14″x4″ square tiers, ice white and assemble, using 10½″ pillars and 12″ round separator plates. Top tier is not cake but a 12″x4″ styrofoam dummy, hollowed to leave walls about 1½″ thick. Line it with foil to keep light from shining through when fountain is inserted.

To decorate: pipe tube 352 ruffled garlands around base of 18″ tier. Over garlands, drape two rows tube 4 stringwork and top with bows. On 14″ tier, pipe tube 320 reverse shell border around base, then starting midway up tier, drap tube 14 zigzag garlands. Drop tube 4 stringwork over garlands and trim with bows. Now, drop tube 4 stringwork from top edge of tier and connect with scallops of tube 4 beading along top. Pipe tube 14 shell border around separator plate.

Next, pipe tube 14 reverse shell border

around base of dummy tier at top. Drop a row of tube 14 garlands around side and cover with tube 3 stringwork, trimmed with bows. Drop tube 3 stringwork from top edge of this tier. Set fountain inside dummy and pipe dots of icing to secure roses on top edge. Pipe tube 65 leaves.

Now attach roses to lower tiers with dots of icing, arranging garlands of roses and buds on bottom tier. Place a rose between each garland on 18″ tier, and attach small plastic bells on 14″ tier. Place Wedding Bell ornament and trim with roses and leaves. Serves 260.

SUMMERTIME
shown on page 51

An elegant cake, simply decorated and embellished with fresh garden flowers.

Bake 14″ square, 10″ round and 6″ round cakes and ice. Assemble on foil-covered board edged with Tuk-N-Ruffle. Pipe white tube 21 shell border around base of all three tiers. Put a 1″ stripe of green icing down to the tip of a decorating cone fitted with tube 21; fill with white icing and pipe curved and modified "e" motion scrollwork.

Insert Flower Spikes into cake and fill with water, using an eye dropper. Arrange flowers. Serves 162.

LAVENDER
Shown on page 50.

First make tube 225 and tube 35 drop flowers, with tube 2 centers. Mount some flowers on florists' wire with icing.

Bake, ice and assemble three square tiers, 12″x4″, 8″x4″ and 6″x3″ on a 13″ plate. Use 5″ Grecian pillars and 9″ separator plate between bottom and middle tiers, 3″ pillars and 7″ plate between middle and top. Pipe tube 22 ball border around base of bottom tier, and over that pipe tube 5 fleur-de-lis with tube 5 balls. Pipe tube 9 ball border around top of bottom tier.

Next, pipe a tube 45 flat strip along edge of separator plates on both 6″ and 8″ tiers, to mask scallops on plates. Pipe tube 10 ball border around base of 8″ tier and tube 9 ball border around top of this tier and base of 6″ tier. Pipe tube 7 ball border around top of 6″ tier.

Place all ornaments on cake before making loops. Pipe mound of icing on top of 12″ tier and place Petite Bridal Couple, arranging flowers around them.

Cut a small styrofoam circle, cover it with green icing and pipe tube 6 beading around base. Insert wired flowers and pipe tube 65 leaves. Set this posy on mound of icing on middle tier. Place Celestial Twins on top of cake and trim with small drop flowers, using icing "glue". Pipe mounds of icing at corners of each tier and attach drop flowers. Pipe tube 65 leaves.

Now add loops of lavender icing with tube 1. Mark center of 12″ tier and drop four loops from each side of this mark,

not allowing loops to touch cake. From this row of eight loops, drop seven, then six, five, and so on down to one. Repeat on all four sides of this tier. On middle tier, start with six loops and go down to one; on top tier, start with four. From each corner of 8″ tier, drop two sections of loops, starting with six loops in each. Drop two sections of four loops each from each corner of top tier. Serves 122.

OVERTURE
Shown on page 54

A stately bridal cake with mini-tier duplicate to serve on the first anniversary.

First bake 3 round tiers, 16″x4″, 12″x4″ and 8″x3″, each two layers. Also, bake a complete set of round mini-tier cakes. Ice all cakes pale yellow.

Assemble the mini-tier cakes and set on a 9″ cake board trimmed with Tuk-N-Ruffle. Pipe tube 22 shell border around base of each tier. Pipe tube 79 lily of the valley blossoms, tube 68 leaves and tube 2 stems around each tier. Drop tube 2 stringwork from separator plate of top tier. Place two small doves between pillars and set Petite Bridal Couple on top.

Now assemble the large cake, using arched pillar separator set below and 5″ Grecian pillars with 10″ separator plates between second and top tier. Pipe a tube 22 shell border around top and bottom of 16″ tier and around base of other tiers.

Pipe tube 79 lily of the valley blossoms, tube 68 leaves and tube 2 stems around each tier. Drop a row of tube 2 stringwork from bottom of top separator plate. Place Cherub Fountain between pillars and trim with tube 68 leaves. Place regular-size Bridal Couple on heart base on top of cake. Serves 215; mini-tier duplicate serves 12.

ALLEGRO
shown on page 55

Subtle color contrast and a lavish use of filigree give this cake a fragile beauty.

Using patterns, make filigree pieces with tube 2 (they are fragile, so make extras in case of breakage.). Edge lattice with tube 2, then finish *all curved edges* of lattice with tube 14 scrolls. Dry.

Make flowers ahead and dry. Pipe tube 217 and tube 224 flowers with tube 1 centers. Then make California poppies. Press foil halfway into ¼″ lily nail, use stiff royal icing and tube 103. Touch center, pull icing over edge, straight across, back to center for square, cupped petals. Smooth and fill centers with damp brush. Add dot of icing in center to hold artificial stamens (tops cut and brushed with icing). Mount some poppies on wire.

Bake, ice and assemble three hexagon tiers, 15″ x 4″, 12″ x 4″ and 9″ x 4″. Use 9″ hexagon separator plates and six 5″ Grecian Pillars. Pipe tube 16 shell borders on all tiers. On 9″ and 15″ tiers pipe border down side of cake at angles, also. Using patterns as guides, pipe thread-like

poppy leaves on sides of 9″ and 15″ tiers. Carefully set filigree pieces in place and secure with dots of icing. Be sure to line up filigree at corners of 9″ and 15″ tiers. Pipe tube 14 shell borders at straight sides and base of filigree on 9″ and 15″ tiers. Attach flowers to sides of 9″ and 15″ tiers with icing, and to filigree on 12″ tier.

Make a little nosegay of wired poppies, twisting stems together. Frame nosegay with a strip of gathered yellow tulle and place on separator plate.

Center top tier with Celestial Twins ornament and trim with flowers. Trim all drop flowers with tube 65 leaves and pipe tube 2 leaves for poppies on top of top tier. Serves 138.

AZALEA
shown on page 56

A strikingly simple and romantic cake.

First make hearts from summer coating in Heart candy molds. Next, bake 3 round tiers, 16″ x 4″, 12″ x 4″ and 8″ x 3″ and ice. Assemble with 5″ Grecian pillars and 10″ separator plates.

All decorating is done in white. Pipe tube 32 shell borders around base and top of each tier. On the two lower tiers, use Pattern Presses to mark scroll designs. Next, outline the scrolls with tube 16. On top tier, pipe tube 16 fleur-de-lis designs around base above border. Secure hearts to sides of cake with dots of icing. Top cake with Lovers In Lace ornament and place fresh azalea bouquet within pillars. Serves 215.

AUTUMN GLORY
shown on page 107

The beauty of nature enchantingly captured in a glowing wedding cake.

In advance, make maple leaves using Color Flow method. Trace a real leaf or use pattern, and tape clear plastic over it so it is wrinkle-free. Tint softened Color Flow icing in autumn colors. Fill decorating cone half full and cut a very small opening. Outline and fill in leaf, then quickly pull out points with small, damp artist's brush. Carefully lift wet leaf from plastic wrap and place inside or over Flower Former to dry. Tint white, cloth-covered florist wire a copper color for stems. Dry and attach to back of each leaf with dot of matching, unsoftened Color Flow icing. Draw veins with brown food color.

Next, bake four cake tiers: one 18″ x 4″ square and three round—14″ x 4″, 10″ x 4″ and 6″ x 3″. Ice and assemble with 12″ plates and 10½″ Roman pillars. Pipe tube 347 circular shell border around base of 18″ tier, and drape tube 320 garland around side. Over the garland, pipe double row of tube 3 stringwork and finish each drape with small bow. Add tube 3 dots above each drape. Use tube 604 for top border. Pipe a tube 8 ball border around base of 14″ tier and tube 364 reverse shell
Continued on page 70

AUTUMN GLORY *Continued*

border around top. Pipe tube 347 zigzag curve around side.

On 10″ tier, pipe tube 364 bulb border around base and tube 364 shell border around top. Drape tube 4 garland around side of tier and top with tube 3 stringwork. Accent each drape with a tube 3 fleur-de-lis and dots in graduated sizes.

Decorate 6″ tier with a tube 364 bulb border around base and add a row of tube 5 fleur-de-lis just above. Drape tube 4 garlands around side of tier and top with 3 rows of tube 3 stringwork. Pipe tube 17 shell border around top. Arrange leaves around petite Bridal couple on 3½″ Heart base. Set Charlemagne ornament on top of cake. Place leaves on all tiers, affixing each with a dot of icing. Serves 320.

CHRISTMAS TRADITION
shown on page 125

A lavish, pure white cake for the bride who wants a formal, beautiful wedding.

First make about 300 sweet peas with tube 103 and set aside to dry. Bake and ice three square tiers, 16″ x 4″, 12″ x 4″ and 8″ x 3″. Assemble with 5″ Grecian Pillars and 13″ square separator plates between base and middle tiers. Use Angel Pillars and 9″ square separator plates between middle and top tiers. Pipe tube 508 star border around base of all three tiers and drape with tube 3 string.

On 16″ base cake, make "i" motion curved garlands with tube 16. Drape tube 3 string over garlands. Attach Angel with Horn and Angel with Violin on each side of tier with icing. On top of tier, make looped scallops to connect side garlands with tube 13. Edge 13″ separator plate with same tube.

On 12″ tier, pipe tube 21 shell border at top edge. Cut "heart" design from grease-proof paper, and trace onto sides of tire. Using "i" motion, pipe heart design with tube 13. Attach Angelinos within hearts with icing.

On 8″ tier, pipe "i" motion curved garlands at sides with tube 15 and drape a line of tube 3 string over garland. Pipe top shell border with tube 18.

Now trim the cake with sweet peas. Pipe heavy lines of icing on two top tiers and press in flowers. Pipe big curve of icing on base tier and attach more flowers. Set four Love's Doves ornaments on 13″ separator plates. Circle pillars with sweet peas.

Gather tulle around four 2″ Glitter Lace Bells and four 3″ bells. Place on separator plates. Gather more tulle and glue within bells of Heavenly Bells ornament. Set ornament on top tier. Serves 230.

BIRTHDAY CAKES (continued)
shown on page 80

NASTURTIUM CAKE. In advance, make nasturtiums on lily nail, using tube 103 for petals and tube 3 for centers.

Bake a 9″ x 4″ hexagon cake and ice. With a toothpick, mark curved guidelines for scrolls on each of 6 side panels of cake. Next pipe tube 2 messages on these panels. To make lattice, drop diagonal lines of tube 2 stringwork from top edge of cake to mark. After finishing first diagonals, go back to starting point and drop lines in opposite direction until lattice is complete. Pipe scrolls with tube 16, repeating for each panel. Now pipe tube 16 shell borders, first around base of cake and then around top. Push candle into center of cake, surround it with a mound of icing and arrange nasturtiums. Complete with tube 65 leaves. Serves 12.

MARIGOLD CAKE. Make marigolds ahead, using tube 101s petals, tubes 12 and 13 for centers. Let flowers dry.

Bake and ice 8″ x 4″ square cake. Pipe tube 21 shell border around base of cake. Drape 3 rows of tube 2 stringwork from top of cake, then pipe a tube 19 shell border around top. Pipe tube 67 leaves at point of each drape. Arrange marigolds on cake top and trim with tube 67 leaves. Next pipe message in script on top of cake, using tube 3. Insert Push-in Candle Holders and insert candles. Finally, put Old Fashioned Fence around cake, securing "posts" with icing. Serves 12.

ZINNIA CAKE. A little gem of a birthday cake trimmed with the button zinnia. Read "how to" section starting on page 90 and make zinnias ahead.

Using the round Mini-Tier set, bake, ice and assemble the three tiers. Pipe tube 21 puff border around base of lower tier, and tube 16 borders around bases of two top tiers. Drape tube 2 strings across each puff on bottom border and add a tube 16 star at point of each drape. Drop tube 2 stringwork loops from top edge of each tier, and finish with tube 16 stars. Arrange zinnias on each tier and at base of cake. Trim with tube 65 leaves. Place candles on cake top and arrange zinnias around them. As a final touch, drop tube 2 stringwork from bases of top two tiers. Serves 12.

PORTRAIT (continued)
shown on page 59

side.) Pipe tube 14 rosettes at point, center and end of fan. Next drop 2 stringwork from rosettes at point of fan to center rosettes, and from center to end. Accent with tube 14 stars. Pipe tube 16 star border at top.

Attach silhouettes to side panels, mounding on icing so they stand out. Pipe tube 8 stems and set easel on top of cake. Place carnations. Pipe tube 65 leaves. Serves 24.

WEDDING BELLS
Shown on page 63

Beautiful for a bridal shower or even a family-only wedding! Serves 12.

Begin by piping pink icing roses making three roses with tube 104 and two with tube 103. Set aside while you prepare a two-layer white or pound cake, 8″ round and 3″ high. Ice in buttercream as smoothly as possible. When icing has set, cover top edge of cake with wax paper and press to give rounded "Australian" look.

Now take a strip of greaseproof paper 3″ high and long enough to fit around the cake sides and fold it into 16ths. (About 1½″ wide sections.) Begin at folded side about ½″ from bottom and cut half a bell shape 1″ in width attached to a ½″ joining strip. Unfold and you will have a chain of eight 2″ wide bell shapes with 1″ joining strips. Pin around cake sides and trace.

First use tube 16 to circle base of cake with dainty shells, then use tube 2 for all the rest of decorating. Pipe beading to form sides of bell shapes, curving garlands of beads between bells at same time. Next, pipe first line of icing at bell bottoms. Overpipe 4 times and then add stringwork, referring to directions given for Australian extension work on page 63. Finish bottom of bells with more beads, reserving space at center for "clapper". Pipe this with same tube, but stronger pressure. With bells complete, add double drape of stringwork between them, and heart-shaped bow and streamers. Add a mound of icing and tube 5 vines and position roses. Pipe tube 65 leaves and your pretty Australian-look cake is ready to delight guests.

LOVE TO MOTHER
shown on page 45

A very feminine cake for your best girl—swagged with ribbons and trimmed with dainty polka dots.

Before starting to decorate, make tube 225 drop flowers with tube 2 centers and dry. Now bake, ice, and assemble the tiers —a 12″ x 14″ 2-layer tier and a 2-layer 9″ heart cake. Pipe a tube 12 ball border at base of 12″ cake and accent with tube 8 dots. Do the same at base of heart cake using tubes 10 and 5.

Mark top edge of heart into 10 equal areas, 5 on each curved side. Pipe a zigzag scallop with tube 16 from mark to mark and drop a tube 104 drape over it. Pipe a tube 104 bow at point of heart. Add tube 2 script message. Mark each side of square cake into 4 equal quarters and pipe same side border as on heart cake. Fill in space between borders with tube 5 polka dots. Pipe tube 104 bows at corners of square cake. Attach a drop flower at each point of side borders with icing. Place Love's Doves ornament on heart cake and trim with flowers. Serves 48.

DECORATING FOR
PROFIT

THE DREAM of almost every decorator is to some day sell their beautiful cakes. Here are letters from readers who made that dream come true.

One of our younger readers is **Lowell Morton** of Lorain, O. Now 17, he began baking at age 9, but didn't get into cake decorating for several years. "When my parents' anniversary came up, I remembered a cake I'd seen with roses. A neighbor lent me the Wilton Yearbook and gave me some excellent icing recipes. I tried decorating and loved it!" After decorating many cakes, Lowell began to receive orders. He is active in his school band and orchestra and sometimes plays organ for a wedding as well as decorating the cake.

Another young man who took up cake decorating about 2 years ago is **Andrew De Putron** of West Deptford, N.J. He specializes in birthday, shower, or "anytime" cakes. Andrew gets many orders and says, "I figure the price of the cake by the materials, any extra additions, and the time."

A high school student who's built up a business selling cakes at school is **Carolyn D'Amour,** West Terre Haute, Ind. Carolyn and a friend decorate cakes at home and sell chances on them, 10¢ each or 3 for 25¢, making about $10 on each cake. She continues, "During the summer I work at a pizza place my father owns, he lets me sell cakes there. I usually make $6 a cake."

Gloria De Hoyos, San Antonio, Tex. started cooking and baking at age 10, and at 25 is decorating for profit. "Since I do not work outside my home, I had some calling cards printed. When I make a cake for a friend or relative I give them my card to give anyone who sees the cake and likes it."

Cards are also a good publicity idea for **Mrs. Jack D. O'Brien** of Sterling Park, Va. "I had business cards made giving my business name, address and phone number. These I give to each new customer.

People are more likely to keep a business card than clip an ad."

Toni Bradford, Melbourne, Ky. has a different way of spreading the word. "The neighborhood grocer suggested I put some cakes in his frozen food section. I make one-layer cakes in disposable pans, decorated with Happy Birthday or the current holiday theme, and they sell for $2.00. He has ready-to-go cakes, and I get good advertising with my name and phone number included with the cake."

"Anyone wanting more business should call a local industry and offer their services; taking a sample cake to the personnel manager might be a good idea," writes **Mrs. Kenneth Warneke,** St. Helens, Ore. She decorates many cakes for employees of the paper mill where her husband worked for many years.

Marjorie McDonald, Panorama City, Cal. who took the Wilton course in 1971, sells many cakes through her church and through the market where she works. Also, some large country clubs nearby have wedding hostesses who refer brides to her. "I work all day at the market, bake and decorate in the evening. This enabled me to take a trip to the Holy Land with my profits." Marjorie does all advertising by word-of-mouth. She charges $75 per 100 servings, plus cost of ornaments, and will deliver, cut and serve wedding cakes at no extra cost.

From **Linda Perkins,** Fort Edward, N.Y., these advertising suggestions, "I send out cards to girls whose engagements are announced in the paper. I also bake for two hotel restaurants that hold receptions.

The most novel advertising is done by **Karen R. Hoffbauer,** Staplehurst, Neb. "Many small towns around here have parades and festivals in summer. To advertise my cake business my father, husband, brother-in-law and I ride unicycles in the

parades. Along with signs about my business we have balls and pens to throw to the people."

Thelma Schmidt of Citrus Springs, Fla. writes, "I have not advertised as yet." Still, she is busy making birthday, luncheon and anniversary cakes for sale. She adds, "I never dreamed that at the age of 50 I would be starting a business of my own! For pricing my cakes, I figure my cost and double it. On wedding cakes I figure 55¢ per serving but I've been told it should be a little more."

"My price for wedding cakes depends on the size and the amount of decoration", writes **Beatrice Davis** of Los Angeles, Cal. "I charge a $20 deposit on all wedding cakes. I deliver and set up the cake. They buy their ornament and I charge a $5 deposit on my cake board, plates and pillars which I refund when they return them. I charge $12 for doll cakes, $11 for small sheet cakes, $18 for large sheet cakes with roses. Any extra decoration I have to buy is charged."

Retired people often find a new way of life in cake decorating. **Iva M. Adkins,** Natchitoches, La., began to decorate about 15 years ago, teaching herself from Modern Cake Decorating and other Wilton books. Retired at age 63, she's now 70 and has a profitable business she can enjoy at home. "I make 2 to 6 wedding cakes every week besides birthday, anniversary, German chocolate and other cakes, and 25 to 30 dozen petits fours a week. I've baked wedding cakes for as many as 500. I love my work and it's so good for anybody as old as I am to have something to do and a nice income. My children are so proud!"

Hazel M. Garey, APO San Francisco, is a serviceman's wife who took decorating classes when she arrived in Okinawa. "Even before I finished classes I was baking and decorating cakes for showers, birthdays and weddings. As soon as we return to the states I plan to have my own little bake shop, baking cakes, selling Wilton supplies and teaching."

Gloria Ayars, the wife of a Navy man in Coco Solo, Canal Zone, explains, "military wives are always looking for something to occupy those long hours when their husbands are working." After cake decorating lessons, she adds, "I have never had to advertise, my cakes advertise for me. I recommend cake decorating to everyone; I find nothing as interesting and enjoyable —and profitable, too!"

While many who decorate for profit learned through classes at the Y or local night schools, a large number are self-taught, using Wilton books. "The Wilton Company put the desire to become a decorator in me, when I ordered my first yearbook in 1970. I was fascinated! Hard as I tried, I just couldn't make roses, so I de-

DECORATING FOR PROFIT
(continued)

cided to take a course. Next thing I knew, I was in business. I show pictures of my cakes and give out calling cards. Someday I hope to have a small shop and someday I hope to take the Wilton Course," writes **Jacqueline Smith,** Lexington, N.C.

Decorators' prices vary according to local custom, but there are some similar rates in the letters we receive. "For birthday cakes, I total all expenses, then triple it to arrive at my price. I do not charge for candles, drop flowers or delivery. For wedding cakes, I charge 55¢ a serving, $3 rental for separator plates and pillars and give each bride a free gift. I charge $5 for Color Flow work and give extras to the customer." is the report from **Mrs. A. J. Parks, Jr.,** Salinas, Cal.

Bonnie Curasi, Millersville, Md., who just started decorating for profit, writes, "I usually charge a set fee of $5 above the cost of the ingredients of my homemade-recipe cakes. I have gotten lots of great ideas from the Wilton books and look forward to CELEBRATE! II".

Sue Hoge, West Islip, N.Y. recalls, "My first wedding cake I sold for $15 because I thought that was enough. Now I receive $55 for the same cake. I could not have done as well without your Wilton books and CELEBRATE!"

"I have found that prospective customers like to have an estimated cost of the cake before they make their decision," writes **Eileen Morefield,** Blytheville, AFB, Ark. She made a file with pictures of her cakes, and a card for each with details of size, color, costs, etc. Most of her customers come by word of mouth.

Gloria L. Wiersema, Middleville, Mich., writes, "For my wedding cakes, I charge $27.50 per 100 servings, $4 per separator, and a $5 delivery and set-up fee."

Jennifer D'Aoust of Detroit, Mich. who is fairly new in the decorating business, tells us, "My prices vary according to what each customer wants. Usually, I charge 3 times cost of ingredients. That keeps me ahead of the rising and falling price of sugar and cake mixes. If they want any ornaments, that's extra." In the same price range is **Brenda Staggs,** VAFB, California, who says, "I usually triple my costs, which allows money for my time and effort. Only

the plastic accessories and Color Flow add to the price."

Catherine Wanniski of Pottsville, Pa., who bakes mostly specialty cakes, says, "For the doll cakes I receive $8, for the bride-and-bridesmaids (baked in small Wonder Mold pans and set on a sheet cake) I get $25, for book cakes $10." Another creator of specialty cakes is **Maria Martinez,** Carpentersville, Ill. who began by baking for her family of 13! "Later I began to attract customers by making my cakes both delicious and pretty. I charge $60 for a wedding cake, $35 for a special baby shower cake with basket of flowers on top, $15 for two 12" layers with trim."

Baking is a family tradition with **Pam Larson,** Liberty, Mo. whose father ran a bakery for 29 years. "For a 2-layer, 6" round cake I charge $6, each size thereafter increases by $1. For wedding cakes, the total number of inches is multiplied by $1.25. A 3-tier cake, 6", 8" and 10" is $30. I charge extra for delivery. I sell Color Flow pieces for $1-$2 depending on size and colors used, small royal icing decorations for cupcakes, usually 8¢ each. I try to fight inflation by not raising prices."

Clydeene Harper of Booker, Tex., works in cooperation with a friend, sharing pans and other equipment. She says, "we charge $8 per cake mix used to bake a wedding or special cake."

Cynthia Schumacher, Boone, Ia., does some cakes but most of her business is in decorated cookies. "Last Christmas I baked and decorated 140 dozen!

Mrs. Dale Snyder, Wahoo, Neb., says, "State law prohibits me having set prices until I have my own bake shop, but I can work on donations. I simply tell customers what others pay. 9", $4.50-$5.00; 10" $6 to $8; 12", $12.00. Wedding cakes are something else; we agree to the price before I make it, but I usually get double the cost of ingredients to cover my labor."

JoAnn Luckey of Winfield, Ill. writes, "I have graduated from small birthday cakes to wedding cakes that serve 200, plus teaching mini-courses in decorating to 8th grade girls at my daughter's school. Now I'm not only earning extra money while staying home with my daughters but I'm sharing the wonderful experience of decorating the Wilton way!"

Janice Smith, Gore, Virginia, writes, "For other women who want a profitable hobby, I have some advertising suggestions. When there is going to be a bake sale in your area, call and tell them you'd like to donate a cake. In return they will give your name and phone number to those who might want to order a cake."

Andrew Griffin of Springfield, Mo., sends a long, helpful letter which we are summing up. "A word of advice to all decorators who want to start a profitable

business. Be sure to ask your local Board of Health or Sanitation Officer for all regulations on selling and handling food. These requirements vary from state to state and it is necessary to know them before your plans go too far."

Kathy Ann Raven of Bolingbrook, Illinois, gives an ingenious fund-raising idea with a business-building side effect. Shortly after moving to a new community, Kathy called the pastor or her church and "volunteered a cake a month to any parish group that cared to raffle it . . ." The offer was taken and soon the calls for other special cakes followed. It wasn't long before "this mother of two toddlers had all the cake orders she could handle"!

ONCE-UPON-A-TIME CAKES
continued from page 111

and decorated in the same manner as Peter and his wife, above. His collar and cuffs are piped with tube 102. His horn is figure piped with tube 7, then outlined with tube 1. Make drop flowers in advance with tubes 193 and 225.

Bake and ice a Wonder Mold cake. Put "hay" all over it with tube 233, starting at bottom and moving in random fashion to the top. Scatter drop flowers and attach Boy Blue to side with icing. Serves 12.

GOLDILOCKS and the Three Bears come to life on your table! Goldilocks is baked in a Blossom pan and uses a small doll pick. Papa and Mama are baked in the Panda pan and Baby Bear in the Panda Chocolate Mold. Before starting to decorate, make a recipe of gum paste (page 32) to use for aprons and buttons. Make tube 131 and tube 14 drop flowers.

Set the Blossom cake on an ornament base, insert doll pick and brush thinned icing over skirt. Pipe a tube 104 ruffle at bottom of skirt, edged with tube 14 shells. Cover bodice with tube 14 stars and trim with a tube 2 bow.

Outline all areas on bear cakes with tube 3. Ice bottom of feet with softened icing. Cover big bears with tube 18 stars, Baby Bear with tube 15 stars. Fill in eyes and noses with softened icing and glaze with corn syrup when dry. Trim Baby's bib with tiny drop flowers and tube 65s leaves.

Now roll out gum paste, cut out Goldilocks' apron from pattern and attach to her waist with icing. Add narrow strip of gum paste for waist band. Do Mama Bear's apron the same way. Also cut out buttons for Papa Bear and make a gum paste bow for Baby's bib. When gumpaste dries, decorate Mama's apron with tube 2 and Goldilocks' with flowers and tube 65s leaves. Attach buttons to Papa's pants with icing.

Set bears on a platter spread with tinted coconut "grass" and drop flowers. Goldilocks stands safely nearby. Serves 26, but who could consider eating them?

Create a portrait cake to honor Thomas Jefferson- author, architect, patriot and president. Directions on page 65.

We hold these truths to be self evident...

1801 ~ 1809

THOMAS JEFFERSON

Celebrate!®

SALUTE OUR COUNTRY'S BIRTHDAY IN JULY AND AUGUST

Americana: the POPCORN WAGON

EXCEPT for the colorful Big Tent circus, the spic and span popcorn wagon of a half century ago probably conjures up more pleasant memories than any treasured piece of Americana. The gleaming brass trim, the spotless windows, the shrill peanut whistle are all memorable to anyone who has ever bought freshly popped and buttered corn at the open window of this elegant equipage. We've re-created it in Color Flow with a realistic 3D effect.

Make the various parts of the wagon at least 48 hours in advance, or longer, so they will dry thoroughly. Tape patterns on cardboard, covering with wax paper or clear plastic wrap, securely taped. Make all outlines in white Color Flow icing with tube 2. Let dry an hour or two, then flow in colors with softened Color Flow icing. Pipe wheels in yellow, using tube 8 for rims and tube 4 for spokes. When dry, peel off paper carefully. Do lettering with tube 1s.

Now, bake a 10" x 3" cake and ice white. Pipe in popcorn border at top and bottom of cake, using tube 8 white puffs and tube 3 gold trim.

Assemble wagon carefully, using small mounds of icing to secure the pieces. Make mounds about ¼ inch high to create 3-dimensional effect. First, position one back and one front wheel on cake. Next comes the blue section, the back of the wagon, then the red roof portion with the top ventilator. Add the blue section of the roof, followed by the popcorn machine. Pipe in popcorn with tube 2. The main red section of the front comes next, after which add the blue gear wheels, gold trim pieces such as whistle, the inside gears and awning hooks at top. Add popcorn sign and other accessories. The awning goes on next, and finally two remaining wheels.

Americana: the PATRIOTIC MIRROR

HERE IS A REPLICA of the charming "bull's eye" mirrors, topped by an American eagle, which adorned Victorian parlors.

First, make mirror of gum paste, using recipe on page 32. It should be rolled about ⅛" thick and dried inside a large mixing bowl, so it assumes watch crystal shape. Let dry 24 hours. Then paint numbers on surface with fine brush and thinned Color Flow icing. Follow pattern. When numbers dry, glaze with corn syrup.

Now make frame, using patterns and Color Flow icing. Outline edge of lower frame with tube 3 and build up upper frame with tube 6, letting icing flow heavily. Tape pattern for scrolls to cardboard, cover with clear plastic taped smooth. Outline with tube 3. Do same with patterns for banner, shield, olive branches and eagle, and outline with tube 2. Pipe roping and tassels on banner with tube 1. Flow icing in appropriate colors. When dry, build up eagle with tube 2, using cut leaf bag for feathers. Build up scrolls with tubes 2, 4 and 6. Attach star to oval with dot of icing.

Next bake 2-tier oval cake and ice white. Pipe tube 4 puff border around base, using circular motion. Add tube 2 scroll as shown. Pipe tube 4 Colonial scroll as around side of cake and finish with tube 2 trim. Pipe tube 4 bulb border around top edge of cake.

To assemble mirror: center it on top of cake. Place frame over it and secure with icing. Pipe tube 4 beading around inside rim. Place banners on lower portion of frame and secure with icing. Set clusters of olive branches over shield and banners. Now position scrolls at top of mirror and place oval and star below eagle. Use mound of icing on a cut down sugar cube to support eagle at proper level. Serves 12.

MAKERS
of
AMERICA

ENGLAND

THE AMERICAN COLONIES, first peopled mainly by English emigrants, were under the rule of England for 168 years. Thus, English ways are deeply woven into the fabric of American culture.

Most Americans are still fascinated by the British flair for pageantry. Nowhere is this flair more beautifully demonstrated than in the dramatic ceremony for the coronation of England's kings and queens.

The glittering gems that symbolize the monarchy are on permanent display in the Tower of London, a medieval castle preserved in the heart of that great city.

The jewels used in the British Coronation decorate this cake honoring our English forebears. We've crowned the cake with the British Royal Coat of Arms, and trimmed it with red and white roses, symbols of the two ruling houses, York and Lancaster, that founded the monarchy.

THE BRITISH CROWN JEWELS
as they appear on the cake

The ceremonial swords (back right and left, base tier). As the sovereign who is to be crowned enters Westminster Abbey for the coronation, four swords are carried before him or her—the twin Swords of Justice, the Swords of Mercy and of State.

The Ampulla or bird vessel (back center, base tier). After the sovereign is acclaimed by the assembled throng and given the oath of office, the annointing takes place. Holy oil is brought in the Ampulla.

The Annointing Spoon (back right, top tier). The oil is poured from the Ampulla's beak into the Annointing Spoon, which is then touched to the sovereign's hand, breast and head.

The Golden Spurs (back left, top tier). The first royal robes are put on and the Golden Spurs, signifying knighthood, are touched to the sovereign's heels.

The Jewelled Sword (left front, base tier). The Jewelled Sword is placed in the sovereign's hands, then about the waist, while he or she is admonished to do justice, stop iniquity, protect the Church, reform what is amiss and confirm what is in good order.

The Armills or bracelets (center back, top tier). The Armills or bracelets of sincerity are placed on sovereign's wrists.

The King's Orb (right front, top tier). Signifying the world under the cross, the Orb is placed first in the sovereign's right hand, then on the altar.

The Coronation Ring (left front, top tier). The ring is placed on the third finger, right hand as the "ensign of kingly dignity".

The Sceptre with the Cross (right front, base tier). This sceptre, signifying power and justice and set with the fabled "Star of Africa" diamond, is placed in the sovereign's right hand.

St. Edward's Crown (center front, top tier). At the high point of the ceremony, the Crown of St. Edward is placed on the sovereign's head. The people shout "God save the King" or "Queen", trumpets sound and

a salute of guns is fired at the Tower of London. The monarch goes to a raised throne, signifying that he or she has taken possession of the kingdom.

Crown of State (center front, base tier). After prayers are said, the new king or queen is arrayed in royal purple robes and the heavy St. Edward's Crown is exchanged for the lighter Crown of State. The monarch leaves the Abby for the State Procession past cheering throngs.

THE CORONATION CAKE

A DISPLAY almost as dazzling as the real Crown Jewels! The Jewels, all made in Color Flow, can be removed from the cake before it is sliced, to be treasured long after the party is over.

To fashion this stunning cake, begin by making the red and white roses with tube 104, leaves with tube 65. Attach both to florist wire stems.

For the Crown Jewels, use the patterns in the CELEBRATE! II Pattern Book, outlining each design with tube 1. Fill in the outlined sections. When pieces are dry, add raised detail and beading with unsoftened Color Flow icing and tube 1.

The Coat of Arms is outlined entirely in gold, then filled in. Overpiping of raised designs, lion and unicorn features, unicorn chain and lettering is done with tube 1 and unsoftened Color Flow. Ermine on crowns is "pulled out" into points to give

a furry look. After Coat of Arms is finished and thoroughly dry, secure two popsicle sticks to back with royal icing, letting half of sticks extend beneath it. Then flow softened Color Flow icing over entire back.

Fill in top half of King's Orb a second time for a 3-dimensional effect. Pearls in Crown of State are piped with tube 2.

To give diamonds in crowns, the jewelled sword, the ring and sceptre the proper faceted effect, brush on patches of blue-tinted icing, then when dry, brush on blue color right from bottle. When designs are completed and completely dry, brush clear piping gel over all precious stones to add sparkle. (Let gel pool a bit here and there to add to the diamond-crusted look.)

Pipe a royal icing spike on the back of completed Crown Jewels to make it easier to secure them to cake sides.

Prepare and ice 2 two-layer hexagon tiers, 9" x 3" and 15" x 4". Assemble on foil-covered base.

Now position Jewels on sides of cake tiers. Pipe large dots of icing on reverse sides, so that each piece stands away from cake slightly. Frame base of each tier with tube 501 rosettes.

Position Coat of Arms on cake top, pushing support sticks down to bottom of tier. Arrange roses and leaves in sprays around it, pushing stems into cake also. Cluster more roses and leaves on the bottom tier.

Your Coronation Cake serves 35.

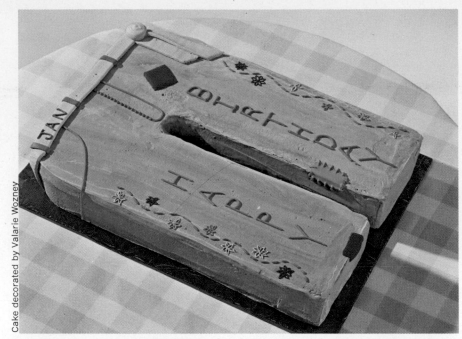

Cake decorated by Valarie Wozney

Cake decorated by Valarie Wozney

CONGRATULATIONS! YOU WON!

Our readers used lots of imagination and some very inventive techniques in decorating these cakes, especially designed to please teen-agers. Here are the happy results, chosen from many good entries.

FIRST PRIZE: BLUE JEANS

Idorea Werner of Highland, Illinois, cut a 9" x 13" sheet cake into the teen-agers' uniform. She lightly mixed two shades of blue icing for a "faded" effect, piped stitching and belt loops and finished off with a colorful sash. We added patches and a touch of embroidery to our reproduction. Sure to please the high school crowd. Congratulations and a $25.00 Gift Certificate to Mrs. Werner.

SECOND PRIZE: TURNED ON!

Helen Wooldridge, APO, New York, wins a $15.00 Gift Certificate for this ingenious creation. The light bulb was made in Color Flow and "plugged in" to the side of the cake. Telephone teen-agers lounge on the top, and the flower trim is hot pink Impatiens. Every parent is familiar with this scene! The CELEBRATE! II staff did wonder if the choice of Impatiens might be a subtle, though not unpleasant, touch.

THIRD PRIZE: THE BUG

Seventeen-year old **Deb Koogman** of Pella, Iowa, manufactured this cake for her boy friend's 18th birthday. Deb stacked three 9" round cakes, cut off about a third to make a straight base, then trimmed the remaining arc for a windshield. Hood and fenders were added from left-over cake and Oreo cookies made the wheels. She added piped bumpers, headlights and "various little parts" with icing. Our reproduction is covered with stars, Deb's was iced smoothly. We're sending Deb a $10 Gift Certificate for a stand-up, stand-out cake, by a teen-ager, for a teen-ager.

HONORABLE MENTION

Three bright decorating ideas won $5.00 Gift Certificates and our congratulations.

Pat Butler, of Penfield, New York, created a Catcher's Mitt cake from a two-layer round cake, used an iced cupcake for the ball. She trimmed the cake for thumb and finger shapes and iced it in chocolate with white stitching.

Barbara Dinger, of Newmanstown, Pennsylvania, trimmed a 9" x 13" cake into the shape of a roller skate, used trimmings for shoe tip and wheels. Skate was covered with stars, sported marshmallow pompoms. Realistic in every detail.

Moni Hourt, of Crawford, Nebraska, decorated a Ball cake as the globe, added eyes and smiling mouth, and set a gum paste graduate's cap on top. Perfect for a "Coming Out" graduation party!

flowers from the garden

ONE OF SUMMER'S special joys is to tend the flower garden and watch the drifts of color appear. Mid-summer's daintiest blossom is the lovely cosmos, borne on slender stems, framed with feathery leaves. Re-create this flower in icing, as a trim for a very festive cake.

First make the cosmos and mount some on wire. (Directions start on page 90.)

Bake, ice and assemble the tiers: 12" x 4" and 6" x 3" petal shapes. Pipe base garland border on 12" cake with tube 504, then frame with tube 13 zigzag. Pipe tube 13 fleur-de-lis at each point of curve. Pipe tube 502 garland at top edge of cake and add tube 13 zigzag frame and fleur-de-lis. Borders for 6" tier are similar, using tube 501 for garlands and tube 13 for frame and fleur-de-lis.

Pipe foliage on cake with tube 1. Stick wired cosmos into tiers and add unwired flowers, attaching with icing. Serves 32.

American Garden Flowers

MANY of the well-loved flowers that bloom in American gardens are not native to the United States, but had their origin in distant parts of the world. The true-blue Bachelor Button came from the Mediterranean, the Nasturtium from Peru and the showy Zinnia from Mexico. The golden Marigold originated in Mexico, was brought to Spain in the early 16th century, then traveled to North Africa and back to Mid- and Northern Europe.

By the mid-eighteenth century all of them were flourishing in the New World. Thomas Jefferson wrote in his journal of planting Marigolds and Nasturtiums in the gardens of Monticello, and for nearly 300 years they have graced the gardens of colonial Williamsburg.

BACHELOR BUTTON CAKE. Make bachelor buttons ahead of time, starting with a tube 7 mound of pale blue icing. With same color icing, pipe a cluster of tube 1 short, pointed dots on top center. With tube 14, and darker blue icing, pull out tiny star petals until mound is covered.

Bake and ice a 9" x 4" heart cake. Pipe a row of tube 21 rosettes around base of cake. Then mark 1" above, and exactly between, each rosette. Pipe a tube 14 star on each mark, and drop tube 3 stringwork from stars to center of rosettes. Now pipe tube 16 star at points of stringwork. Pipe tube 19 stars around top edge of cake. Arrange bachelor buttons on mound of icing on cake top and add tube 66 leaves. Do script message with tube 2, and finally insert Push-in Candle Holders, having first put in candles. Serves 12.

Continued on page 70.

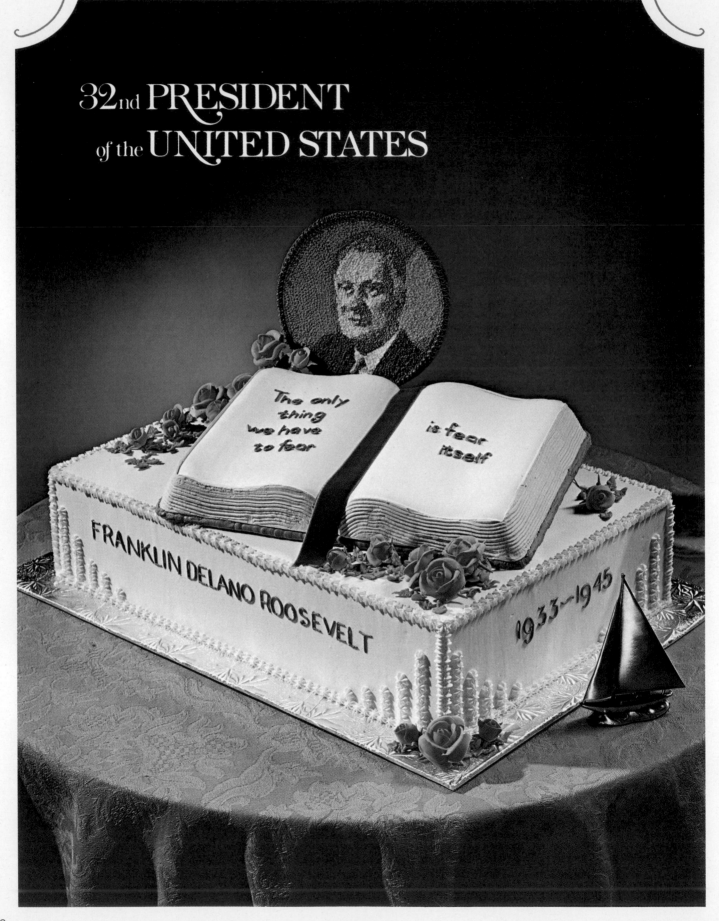

34th PRESIDENT of the UNITED STATES

We, who are free,

must proclaim anew our faith

1953

1961

Decorating directions for both cakes, page 65

START

THINGS

POPPING

WITH OUR

FIRECRACKER

CAKE!

This simple but ingenious cake takes the design of the first American flag and turns it into a firecracker. A sparkling centerpiece for a Bicentennial party!

Bake 5 one-layer cakes, each 6" round. Stack them up, filling lightly with frosting between for a total height of about 10¼". Set on cake board and ice. Push a narrow dowel rod the same height into top all the way to bottom of cake to keep layers steady.

Take a narrow piece of greaseproof paper 10¼" long and draw a line ¾" down from top. Using this as a guide, fold the entire piece of paper, fan style, making each fold same size as top fold. Unfold and you will have 13 equal divisions. Pin to top edge of cake and carefully mark off the spaces on side of cake from top to bottom. If filling between layers makes cake a little higher than 10¼", let bottom division be the largest.

Cut a second piece of greaseproof paper, 4" deep x 4½" wide, position at top edge of cake and mark around with toothpick for blue patch. Remove paper, fold into quarter, open and mark center. Mark dots on folds ¾" in from edge and using these dots as guide, mark a freehand circle of 13 dots. Position on cake again and punch through to mark 13 stars.

Now with tube 18 and red icing, cover entire top of cake with stars closely piped together. Continue down sides, alternating red and white stripes, leaving space marked for patch blank.

With same tube and white icing pipe circle of stars in patch area, then fill in rest of patch with closely piped blue stars. Overpipe white stars again.

Explosion of flares at top of cake is made by taking several lengths of wire, inserting through tube 6 into cones of colored icing, then squeezing while you pull them out again to coat wire. Bend as you pull wire out to get curved effect, then push into styrofoam block to dry. When all coated wires are dry, arrange in top of cake for flare effect. Serves 18.

CHINA

By 1860 only about 30,000 Chinese had come to America, probably because they were not anxious to leave the world's oldest civilization. This cake pays tribute to immigrants from the Far East, now fellow Americans Decorating directions start on page 153.

MAKERS of AMERICA

flag waving cakes

Happy Birthday America

200 years

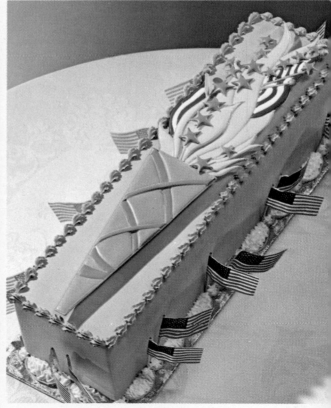

Join our country's celebration with cakes that show your pride! Opposite page: a birthday cake. This page: a cake to honor our first president, a pretty doll whose message is "Keep America beautiful". And a flag-trimmed torch of liberty. Directions for all, page 97.

Above: a fragile winged cake done in the true South African manner. Below: a cake just as lacy and beautiful, decorated in the faster Wilton-American way. Directions for both cakes on facing page.

Cake decorated by Valarie Wozney

88

A CAKE DECORATED

IN THE

MANNER

WHILE THE SOUTH AFRICAN school of cake decorating is strongly influenced by English methods, it has a style all its own. There are three major factors in the South African style: fantastically delicate lacework or filigree; fine modeling of gum paste flowers and marzipan fruits and vegetables; and "run-in work" similar to Color Flow. The latter is used in vivid colors, for three-dimensional scenes.

South African decorators often use geometrical cakes, five, six, or eight-sided, though round cakes are also popular. For special occasions like weddings and anniversaries, they bake dark fruit cake, usually covering it with rolled fondant, then a coat of royal icing, before decorating. Soft cakes are usually reserved for family parties, informal celebrations and children's parties and iced with buttercream.

SOUTH AFRICAN decorators use the icing syringe more than the decorating bag. However, they choose the bag for line, lace and trellis (lattice) work, as it is easier to control for such fine detail. They use the parchment bag also for "run-in work," with just the tip cut and no tube. For "run-in," they use royal icing diluted with water until a spoonful dropped back into the icing disappears without a trace on the count of ten.

Their tubes are similar to ours. They also use the flower nail, and net nails similar to those used in Australian decorating. Many of their recipes call for "pure icing sugar," confectioner's sugar with the cornstarch left out. It can be obtained from any confectioners' supply house. Buttercream

is used mainly for flowers and borders piped directly on the cake. Royal icing is used for flowers and decorations made ahead, and for delicate lattice, line and lace work.

Lace work is such a major part of South African decorating that it deserves special mention. Along with delicately transparent lace wings and other large designs, they make tiny lace points and frills. Ribbon streamers set in deeply sculptured curves are another aspect of South African cakes. Lines are overpiped again and again, a technique called hollow linework.

"Run-in work" is often used by South African decorators to create colorful three-dimensional paintings in curved frames to decorate a cake. Many colors may be used in a single design, so great care is required in piping and assembling the sections of the "painting." Using this picture technique, with a plaque for each side of the cake, South African decorators create "story" cakes with outstanding results.

SOUTH AFRICAN WING CAKE

Well in advance make the four lace wings for corners of cake. Tape CELEBRATE! II patterns to a heavy piece of glass, then cover with wax paper and tape down smoothly. Do all the lace work with tube 00, starting at outer edges and moving in to center. Dry 24 hours, then overpipe major lines of wings. Dry about six hours, then peel off wax paper and overpipe major lines on other side. Make extras, as they are very fragile.

Now make the roses and buds with tubes 103 and 104. Give roses a two-tone effect by piping a rosebud deep yellow, then adding petals in a lighter yellow.

Bake and ice an 8″ x 4″ square cake and ice very smoothly. Mark scallop design on top and sides with toothpick. Working with one section at a time, pipe a series of straight lines with tube 1, from mark on top of cake to mark on side. Start with the second piped line and overpipe once, overpipe the third line twice, the fourth three times and so on until line in center is overpiped nine times. Continue overpiping, decreasing the number of times on each line. This characteristic overpiping gives edges of cake a rounded, "puffy" effect.

When all lines are completed, pipe a tube 1 line on scallop mark on top of cake, then overpipe once. Pipe a tube 1 line on scallop mark on sides of cake and one just below it. Overpipe first line twice, then pipe a row of tiny scallops below lower line. Finish base of cake with tube 22 shells.

Pipe tube 3 stems on top of cake and position roses and buds in a spray. Add tube 3 leaves. Now pipe a thin line of icing on side of cake at corner. Continue on top of cake in true diagonal. Carefully place one wing in place. Pipe tube 2 bulbs on either side of wing. Attach other three wings in same manner. Serves 12.

AN AMERICAN ADAPTATION

The lacy winged look achieved in a time-saving way!

Tape lace patterns to board, tape wax paper smoothly over and pipe lace with tube 1. You will need six large "wings," nine smaller ones, and six each of side lace pieces. Make extras, if you like, to trim board. When lace is thoroughly dry, overpipe main pattern lines. Dry again, turn over and overpipe main lines again.

Bake, ice and assemble a 12″ x 4″ and a 6″ x 3″ hexagon cake. Place on 18″ foil-covered circle. Pipe tube 4 bead border on base of 12″ cake, and tube 3 borders on 6″ tier and top of 12″ tier. Attach lace motifs to sides with dots of icing and add tube 1 dots to edges. Pipe dots of icing on top of 6″ cake and carefully position one lace motif. Place other two pieces, propping till dry. Place lace pieces against corners of 6″ tier, then the 12″ tier, using dots of icing as glue. Attach additional lace pieces to board. Serves 26.

THE GREEN BOUTIQUE

New Flowers and Other Growing Things

TRILLIUM

Refreshing, snow-white flower of spring. Line a lily nail with foil, and insert into block of styrofoam to hold it firm. Using tube 104, with wide end of tube held down against the nail, pipe three narrow petals. At the top of each petal, pipe a wide, slightly flared petal. With damp brush, brush the petals so they join together smoothly. Pinch ends to make a pointed tip on each petal. Dry. Put fresh foil into nail, pipe a tube 3 mound of icing and insert the flower in upright position. Pipe tube 1 yellow stamens. Pipe tube 67 leaves, darker green veins brushed on.

MARSH MARIGOLD

Gleaming gold! Using tube 103, hold decorating bag at right angle to number 7 nail. Have wide end of tube just touching surface and narrow end almost flat. Beginning at center of nail, press out rounded petals, turning nail as you move hand out to edge and back again, curving slightly upward to make cupped shape. With tube 2, pull out spikes in center.

SPRING BEAUTY

Dainty pink flower that grows in natural clusters or "bouquets." Hold wide end of tube 101 against center of flower nail, with narrow end almost flat. Begin at center of nail and press out five petals, turning nail as you move hand out to edge and back. Curve the petal upward to create slightly cupped edge. Paint deep pink stripes on petals with tiny brush. Pipe pink tube 1 dots in pink for stamens.

BELLFLOWER

Nodding little bells of deep blue-violet. Make flower on a cone shape covered with wax paper. Hold tube 103 wide end down, just touching tip of cone, and move hand out and down, then back to tip, to make a slightly flared petal. Pinch tip of petal to a point. Repeat for five petals, leaving tiny hole at center. Make a tiny loop at one end of 20-guage florist wire. When petals are dry, insert wire through hole. Over this loop pipe a tube 2 yellow center, pulling the icing to a point. Pipe a tube 2 green cap around base of each flower and pull out spiky sepals of green from cap.

BUTTON ZINNIA

First pipe a little ring on a number 2 flower nail with tube 3. Cover the ring with tube 101s petals. Repeat the circular rows of petals, lifting each row a little higher to form the domed shape. Fill center with tube 13 stars, add tiny tube 000 stamens.

TRILLIUM

MARSH MARIGOLD

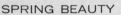

SPRING BEAUTY

BELLFLOWER

BUTTON ZINNIA

COSMOS

White, clear pink or deepest crimson, pipe the cosmos as two flowers. Use tube 104 and a number 13 flower nail. Wide end of tube down, start at center, go out and back, making square shape at tip of petal. Make another petal facing first. Brush centers with damp brush to fill in space. With end of brush, make notches at tips of petals, then brush grooves into center. Now make two more petals the same way in cross effect. Slide wax paper off nail and prop against Flower Former to dry. When dry, attach flower to nail again and pipe four more petals in cross formation on top of first four petals. Center with a flat dot with tube 12, and circle with tube 1 dot stamens. Brush deeper color at center with food color.

CHERRY BLOSSOM

Use tube 101 and a number 4 nail to make this dainty pink blossom with an oriental air. Starting at center, wide end of tube down, press out five rounded petals, overlapping slightly. Pipe a mound in center with tube 2 and insert many ½" artificial stamens.

THISTLE OF SCOTLAND

Pipe on wax paper, taped to board, with royal icing. First pipe three 1" lines of purple icing with tube 2. Now pipe many short, string-like petals to fill in between these lines. Next, pipe a tube 4 bulb of green icing, tapered toward the petals. Keep layering petals to build fluffy shape. Finally, pipe crisscross lines of tube 1 green string over the bulb. For leaves, using green Color Flow icing, not thinned, and tube 70, pipe a long slim leaf on wax paper. While leaf is still wet, pull out tiny points along edges with a damp artist's brush.

SHAMROCK LEAVES

Ireland's emerald emblem! Make the leaf with tube 103 and a number 7 nail. Hold tube at 45° angle, wide end down, touching center of nail. Turn nail and move out to its edge for half petal. Move back to center, out to edge again and back for heart-shaped petal. Repeat for two more petals, then add stem with tube 2.

STALKS OF WHEAT

Use gold royal icing and tube 4. Cut 22-gauge wire into 7" lengths. Force the wires into the bag and pull them out, coating the wires. Set in styrofoam to dry. Lay the wires on wax paper. Starting at tip, pipe bulbs of icing along one side of wire with tube 2 to length of about 1¼". Now make a row of bulbs on other side of wire and finally in center. When dry, turn over and pipe another row of bulbs on back of wire.

COSMOS

CHERRY BLOSSOM

THISTLE OF SCOTLAND

SHAMROCK LEAVES

STALKS OF WHEAT

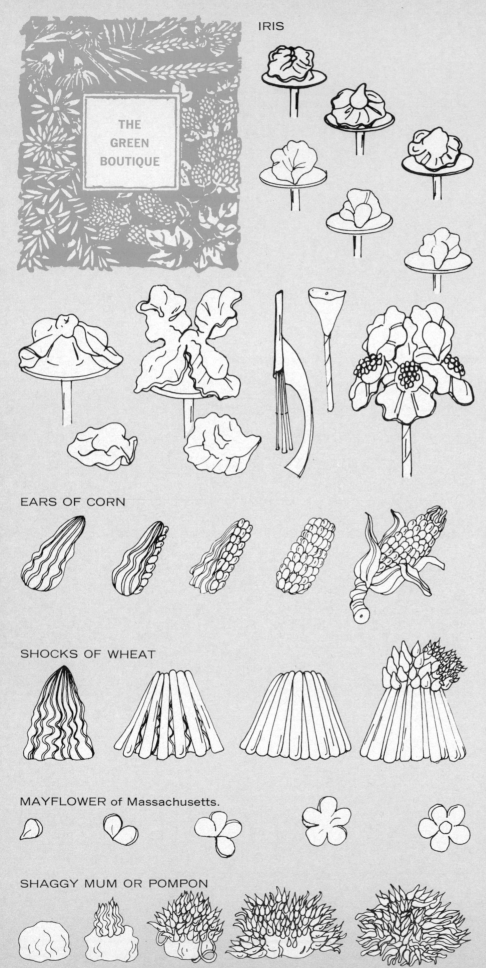

IRIS

THE GREEN BOUTIQUE

EARS OF CORN

SHOCKS OF WHEAT

MAYFLOWER of Massachusetts.

SHAGGY MUM OR POMPON

IRIS

The regal fleur-de-lis of France. To make it quite simply, pipe three ruffled cup-shaped petals that stand upright and three down-curving petals, then assemble.

STEP ONE. Use upper half of a plastic 1⅝" two-piece lily nail as a dome-shaped flower nail. Cover smoothly with foil and, beginning at top, pipe a tube 103 ruffled petal, moving down to edge of nail and back to top.

STEP TWO. Pipe a shell-motion bulb of icing with tube 4 in center of ruffled petal, tapering to a point at petal base. Brush bulb and petal together with a damp brush. Remove foil with petal carefully, and dry. Make 3 down-curved petals.

STEP THREE. Cover nail again and this time begin petal at edge of nail, curving it up and around top edge of dome and back down to nail edge again.

STEP FOUR. Pipe shell-shaped bulb with tube 4 as before, this time tapering at edge of nail. Brush bulb and petal together with damp brush and dry. Make 3 up-curved petals.

STEP FIVE. Cover nail with foil again. Pipe a large dot of icing on tip of each down-curved petal and arrange in circle on nail. Let dry for a few minutes. Then pipe a dot of icing on tip of each up-curved petal and carefully press above down-curved petals, positioning between them. Mount the iris on a wire stem as shown on opposite page, but since it is quite heavy, tape 3 florist wires together for stem. When completely dry, pipe "beards" on lower petals with tube 1 dots.

EARS OF CORN

Very real and dimensional, very fast to do. First pipe a long shell with tube 22 on taped-down wax paper. Fill in with tube 3 "kernals" between each ridge of shell. Add tube 68 out-curved "husks" and a tube 4 stalk. Finish with tube 1 "cornsilk" at tip.

SHOCKS OF WHEAT

Pipe a tube 4B base, tapering to a point on taped-down wax paper. Cover base with tube 7 lines. Let dry, then fill in with more lines, using tube 5. Add tube 5 shell-shapes at top and tube 1 "grains."

MAYFLOWER of Massachusetts.

This little pink flower grows in clusters against a background of glossy pointed leaves. Hold tube 101s flat to surface of flower nail and press out five small round petals. Pipe tube 1 stamens in center.

SHAGGY MUM OR POMPON

Pipe a mound with tube 199 on wax paper. Hold tube 233 straight up and pipe petals on top of mound. Hold tube at 45° angle, move down, and circle mound with more petals, Finally, holding tube almost parallel with paper, cover base of mound. Fast, easy, spectacular!

PUSSY WILLOW

Right on the cake, pipe a curving brown stem with tube 3. Pipe tube 5 bulbs on either side of stem in a pale grey-violet. Below each bulb pipe a tube 65s leaf shape.

SUN FLOWER of Kansas

The golden flower of the sun. Using flower nail number 2, pipe tube 352 petals in a ring, pressing tube to nail, then lifting straight up. While petals dry, pipe a tube 12 brown center on wax paper, flatten, and cover with brown-tinted sugar. When dry, set within ring of petals, attaching with icing. When blossom is dry, turn over and pipe green base. Begin with tube 12 dot in center. Then pipe overlapping points all around with tube 352, lifting as you did for petals. Pipe the bud in three steps—first a green tube 12 cone for base, then tiny tube 65 yellow petals pointing almost straight up, and last, more petals surrounded by green points with same tube. Big leaves are piped with tube 70.

DOGWOOD

For this pink beauty, use tube 103 at a 45° angle with wide end of tube touching center of number 7 nail, narrow end pointed out. Press bag lightly, then increase pressure as you turn nail and move out to its edge for a half petal that fans out slightly. Move straight back to center of nail and right out to edge again to finish petal. Pipe 4 heart-shaped petals in all, brush dip in each heart with green, then brown. Center with tube 2 dots, dry in Flower Former.

PINE CONE

Cover a cone shape with wax paper and smoothly coat with icing to form a base on which to build cone. With tube 97, pipe standing petals at peak just as you would in forming a rose. Pipe 3 near vertical petals at peak in "cup" shape. Pipe 5 petals in next lower tier, constantly moving cone as you would a flower nail. Add 6 petals below them, then another row of seven petals.

HOW TO MOUNT FLOWERS AND LEAVES ON WIRE

STEP ONE. On a wax paper square, pipe a small green icing mound with tube 6.
STEP TWO. Insert green florist wire 6" long into mound and brush smooth. Push bare wire end in styrofoam to dry.
STEP THREE. Remove wax paper and attach flower to mound with icing.
STEP FOUR. For leaves, lay florist wire on wax paper. Pipe leaf directly over wire end, so wire is center vein. For side leaf, let icing build up on wire before pulling to a point. Push wire into styrofoam to dry.

PUSSY WILLOW

SUN FLOWER of Kansas

DOGWOOD

PINE CONE

FLOWERS AND LEAVES ON WIRE

93

CAKE PREPARATION FOR ENGLISH AND AUSTRALIAN METHOD DECORATING

Decorating cakes in elegant English and Australian Methods necessitates specific steps in cake preparation. First, the cake must be firm and moist—fruit cake is ideal. Second, both methods call for a marzipan covering to precede the final icings—royal for English Method cakes, rolled fondant for Australian Method.

Here, we show the step-by-step cake-covering procedures. The cakes used are 8″ x 3″ and each requires doubling the marzipan recipe found on page 96. Before you begin the following steps, fill in any holes or crevices in the cake with marzipan for a smooth, even surface.

ENGLISH METHOD PREPARATION

1. Dust work surface with powdered sugar, then roll out a ball of marzipan to a ¼″ thick circle, slightly larger than the diameter of the cake.

2. Brush cake top with warm apricot glaze, (heat to boiling and strain 1 cup apricot jam). Place cake upside down on marzipan, cut excess edges with a knife; then with a spatula, lift and turn cake upright.

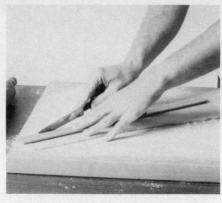

3. Next, shape remaining marzipan into a long narrow roll and flatten with rolling pin. Measure and cut width to equal height of cake, length to slightly exceed circumference.

4. Now, brush cake sides again with apricot glaze, place sideways on one end of marzipan strip and roll, patting marzipan in place until strip ends overlap. Now the cake is ready for a smooth coat of royal icing and decorating in the English Method.

AUSTRALIAN METHOD PREPARATION

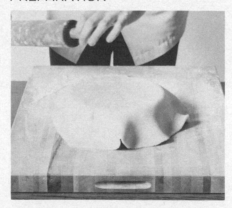

1. Brush cake with apricot glaze as in step 2, above. Dust work surface with powdered sugar and roll out marzipan to ¼″ thick circle large enough in diameter to cover entire cake surface. Fold marzipan over rolling pin, place on edge of cake and unroll marzipan onto cake.

2. Gently press marzipan into place around cake; then cut excess at base. Now the cake has a seamless covering perfect for the rolled fondant icing, characteristic of Australian Method cakes.

ROLLED FONDANT RECIPE

  2 tablespoons Grayslake Gelatin
  2 ounces water
1½ tablespoons glycerine
  4 ounces glucose
  2 pounds powdered sugar

Heat gelatin and water, (do not boil) until gelatin is dissolved. Combine glycerine and glucose in a small bowl and add gelatin mixture when ready. Seive powdered sugar into a large bowl, make a well in the center of sugar and add all liquid ingredients. Stir with a wooden spoon and knead. Tint with food color if desired.

3. To cover cake with fondant, brush marzipan covering with apricot glaze. Then coat work surface with a thin layer of non-stick pan-release and dust with cornstarch. Roll fondant to a ¼″ thick circle large enough in diameter to cover cake surface. Just as you did with marzipan, fold fondant over a rolling pin, place on end of cake and unroll.

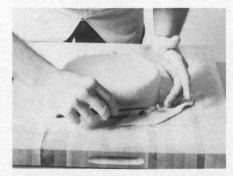

4. Smooth fondant into place, cut off excess at base and the cake is ready for dainty Australian decorating.

A MIDWEST BARN
shown on page 105

True Americana, and a wonderful center-piece for fall parties.

Much of the decorating is done in advance. Make the shocks of wheat and ears of corn according to directions in the Green Boutique, page 90. Pipe the large pumpkins with tube 199 and the smaller ones near the barn with tube 362 and figure-piping technique. Add stems with tube 13 and dry.

Now bake the cakes. The base is a 14" x 4" square, the tier above it is a 10" x 3" square. The barn is built from two 5" x 2" square cakes stacked. To make the roof of the barn, bake two 6" x 2" round cakes. Cut into octagon shapes. Cut octagons in two, and fill and stack three of these halves to form the "hip roof". The silo is baked in a juice can. Fashion the silo roof from light cardboard. Ice all smoothly.

Assemble the two base tiers. Push dowels into 14" tier to support weight above. Push dowels through 10" tier to cake board. Edge tiers with tube 22 shells.

Make ribbon-like trim on barn with tube 44, add details with tube 3. Place barn and silo on 10" tier. Add "hay" around barn with tube 1. Set small wheat shocks and pumpkins around barn.

Attach ears of corn, wheat shocks and larger pumpkins to square tiers. Serves 76.

CHRISTMAS MORNING
shown on page 130

A very large, splendid cake, but decorating is easy if done in steps.

1. PREPARE ALL COLOR FLOW PIECES, using patterns. Gift wagons and "Merry Christmas" are outlined with tube 2, then flowed in. Do 16 or more gift wagons on 16" Cake-side Formers. When dry, trim with tube 2 and pipe tube 14 stars on wheels. Tree ornaments are outlined and trimmed with tube 1.

Make candles for tree by piping a tube 3 line about 1¼" long on wax paper. Brush a line of red paste color inside paper cone fitted with tube 3. Fill bag with yellow icing. Pipe a tube 13 shell at top of each candle for flame.

Pipe holly leaves on wax paper with tube 70 and unthinned Color Flow icing. Immediately pull out points at edge with damp brush. Dry on Flower Formers. Add stem with tube 3 and tube 3 berries.

2. MAKE GARLANDS to hang from Arched Pillar Separator Plate. Cut six 5" pieces of 18-gauge wire. Bend one end of each into small loop. Tape to top of separator plate midway between each pillar, straight ends pointing to center of plate, loop just projecting from edge. Now cut six pieces of the same wire to 11¼". Make a small hook on each end (this will hook onto loops on separator plate). Holding wires against separator plate, bend each into an arc from hook to hook. Lay wires flat on wax paper. Starting at center of each, pipe tube 75 leaves, to completely cover wire, in royal icing. Dry.

3. BAKE THE COOKIES. Cut Jack-in-the-box from dough using pattern. Bake a 4" square cookie for lid of box. Outline color areas on Jack and flow in colors with thinned Color Flow icing. Add features with tubes 2 and 4. "Paint" lid.

4. BAKE THE CAKES. Bake tree cake in 3-D Tree Pan. Two lower tiers are 16" x 4" and 12" x 4" two-layer rounds. Packages above are 8" x 2" square, 6" x 3" x 3" rectangle, a cylinder cake baked in a juice can, about 6" x 3", and a 4" cube cake for box for Jack. Ice all smoothly.

5. ASSEMBLE AND DECORATE. Cover tree cake with tube 16 stars, then pull out tube 75 leaves, starting at base. Attach candles and ornaments with dots of icing. Set tree within Arched Pillar Tier Set.

Assemble 16" and 12" tiers on upper separator plate. Divide top edge of 12" cake into sixths. Drop tube 2 curved guidelines. Starting at center of guidelines, pipe tube 75 leaves to form garland. Pipe tube 32 shell borders at base of 12" and 16" tiers. Pipe reverse shell border with tube 19 at top of 16" tier. Attach gift wagons to sides of 16" tier with icing. Pipe a curve of tube 1 dots between each wagon.

Trim the package cakes. Set 8" square on 12" tier and use tube 44 for ribbon trim, tube 16 star base border. Trim 6" cylinder with tube 44 ribbons and 104 bow. Add tube 32 stars. 6" x 3" rectangle has tube 44 ribbons and tube 14 star base border. Set cylinder and rectangle cakes in position.

Border "box" and lid with tube 2 beading. Attach lid with toothpicks. Set "Jack" in position on mound of icing, prop with toothpicks. Set on top of packages and attach "Merry Christmas" to side of box with icing.

Hang the wired garlands on the separator plate. Garnish with satin bows. Add holly to pillars and packages with icing. The most festive Christmas cake ever! Serves 100.

HERE is an **always-works** recipe that is worth remembering. The HAPPY HOME RECIPE that serves all is provided by **Mrs. W. Westfield,** Bowie, Maryland, follows:

    4 cups Love
    2 cups Loyalty
    3 cups Forgiveness
    1 cup Friendship
    5 spoons Hope
    2 spoons Tenderness
    4 quarts Faith
    1 barrel Laughter
    1 ounce Obedience

Take Love and Laughter, mix it thoroughly with Faith. Blend with Tenderness, Kindness and add Friendship, Hope and Obedience. Sprinkle lavishly with Laughter. Bake with lots of Sunshine. Serve daily in generous helpings.

MODELING WITH
MARZIPAN

This traditional holiday confection is a luscious almond paste mixture that can be tinted and modeled into whimsical figures and wonderfully realistic fruits and vegetables—as easily as modeling clay. Here's how.

MARZIPAN RECIPE.

> 1 cup almond paste (8 ounce can)
> 2 egg whites, unbeaten
> 3 cups confectioners sugar
> ½ teaspoon vanilla or rum flavor

Knead almond paste by hand in bowl. Add egg whites, mix well. Continue kneading as you add sugar, 1 cup at a time and flavoring until marzipan looks like heavy pie dough. Cover with plastic wrap, store tightly sealed in refrigerator and marzipan dough will keep for months. Before using again, let stand at room temperature until soft enough to work. Or soften with a drop or two of warmed corn syrup.

TO TINT before modeling, knead colors into basic mixture, working in one drop of liquid food color at a time until you reach desired shade. For chocolate color and flavor, work in powdered, unsweetened cocoa. If this makes dough too stiff, soften with a little extra egg white or a few drops of corn syrup.

TO PAINT after modeling, dilute food color with any white brandy, such as kirsch, until you reach the shade you want. Then paint on with nearly dry sable brush.

TO GLUE marzipan pieces, touch piece to a sponge soaked in egg white, then fix to second piece with a turning motion.

TO GLAZE marzipan, lightly brush on glaze solution (mix ½ cup corn syrup, 1 cup water, bring to boil). This gives a soft shine. For a high shine, cut water to one or two tablespoons and simply beat.

TOOLS YOU NEED are just an orange stick, sharpened to a point at one end, and a small kitchen knife with a pointed blade.

TO MODEL marzipan is almost as easy as working with modeling clay, but it does take practice. Dust work table and hands with powdered sugar. With palms of hands, roll mixture into a 12″ long cylinder, ⅞″ in diameter. Cut 1″ pieces and, working between heels of hands, roll into smooth balls, then shape these into cones, pear and oval shapes. To keep similar shapes uniform, cut pieces same size and model all at same time.

ROLL marzipan like pie dough, dusting board and rolling pin with powdered sugar.

Dry marzipan figures 48 hours before using.

FRUITS & VEGETABLES

For pumpkins, apples, cherries, grapes and sweet corn, model tinted marzipan mixture into natural shapes, then add indentations. Score or cut grooves with knife blade, make "eyes" with orange stick. (See page 106 for potato directions.) Brush apples with food coloring on damp cloth. Lightly glaze, then add icing stems, leaves. Roll cone-shaped pink dough for strawberries, roll in red-colored granulated sugar.

STANDING FIGURES

Bodies, heads, limbs and trims of all figures are modeled separately, then put together. Use your judgment as to amounts of dough needed for each figure, using diagrams and dimensions given here as a guide. A good plan is to measure off amount needed for the whole figure, roll into a single cylinder, then pinch off portions needed for head, arms and so on. This makes it easier to keep all in proportion. Tint pieces of dough before modeling or paint modeled pieces before assembling. Glaze after assembling.

Standing figures are about 5″ high. Arms and legs are formed of a single cylinder about 5″ long and are rolled thinner at center, so they may be bent in half. Hands are cut into ends of arm cylinder and feet are separate balls of dough, rolled into shoe or boot shapes.

Aprons, belts, collars and kerchiefs are bits of marzipan rolled flat, then cut into shape. Hair, features and details are piped with tube 1.

The girl figure is made of two cone shapes, small bodice atop a larger grooved skirt. Arms are a single cylinder attached around top cone. Boy figure has a single cylinder for arms, another thicker one for legs. Add toothpicks at all joinings for extra support.

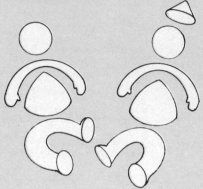

SEATED FIGURES

These are made just the same as the standing figures, except that it is not necessary to roll center of leg cylinders thinner. Just curve legs around to front of figure. Bend "knees" in natural position.

KNEELING FIGURES

Make the same as standing figures, except for same-thickness leg cylinders. Put them into bending attitudes by letting them rest on "hands" or "knees." (In this case, extra pieces of dough should be used for hands.) Bend cylinders back at knees for natural look, and use toothpicks for support and joining.

THE SPIRIT OF AMERICA
shown on front cover

200 YEARS. The life-span of our country. It started with a call to freedom. Near this anniversary mark, American astronauts saw the rise of the beautiful planet Earth as they moved in their space ship toward the moon.

We have adapted the famous painting "The Spirit of '76" by Archibald Willard to adorn the top of this cake. The painting was immensely popular at America's Centennial in 1876. A Color Flow view of the planet Earth completes the base.

Make Color Flow pieces first. Outline "Spirit of '76" and flow in areas. When dry, turn over, lay several popsicle sticks at bottom with ends projecting and flow in again for extra strength. Sticks will support picture when placed on cake. Stars on flag, cords on drum and drumsticks are piped after picture is completed.

Outline and flow in planet Earth. When dry, turn over and flow in again. After final drying, add tiny tube 1 dots, clustering thickly, to land and water areas.

Make tube 104 roses and buds, and tube 67 and 70 leaves. When dry, mount all on florist wire. (See page 93.)

Bake a 12" x 18" and a 9" x 13" sheet cake, chill and cut out "1776" and "1976" shapes, using patterns. Ice smoothly.

Bake and ice a two-layer 18" square cake for base. For second tier, bake one 9" round and one 9" square cake, each two layers. Cut round cake in half and set halves on either side of square cake to make elongated oval. Ice smoothly. Push dowels into rear of square base cake for support, and set oval cake on top.

To decorate the number cakes, pipe tube 46 red and white stripes on lower portions. Pipe thirteen white stars on upper portions with tube 16, then fill in with blue stars. Overpipe white stars. Edge with tube 3 beading.

Pipe tube 32 shell border at base of square cake, and tube 21 shell border at top. Pipe tube 21 scrolls on sides. On oval tier, pipe tube 16 base shell border. Edge top with tube 32 upright shells, and drop tube 2 string drapes.

Now set number cakes on tiers. Position "Spirit of '76" at rear of oval tier, pushing in sticks for support. Place planet Earth on front of square tier on mound of icing. Arrange roses and leaves in sprays and set around cake, attaching with icing. Serves 118 patriots.

☆ ☆ ☆ ☆ ☆ ☆ ☆

KEEP AMERICA BEAUTIFUL
shown on page 87

In advance, make stars for skirt using Color Flow technique. Outline with tube 1 and flow in icing. Make daisies, bachelor buttons and zinnias (see page 90) and mount on wires. "Paint" sprinkling can with white icing, trim with blue.

Next, bake a cake in the Wonder Mold pan, and a 12" x 2" round cake. Ice round cake green and pat with sponge for grass effect. Place smaller cake on top. Insert "little girl" doll pick in cake, placing it so she seems to lean forward slightly. Fill in skirt and pinafore with tube 16 stars and pipe tube 103 ruffles.

To make cap, pipe a mound of icing on doll's head with tube 1A, and flatten it slightly. Use back of brush to make tucked effect. Smooth surface with moistened brush. Edge with tube 104 ruffle. Pipe tube 2 red string bow on cap, and tube 44 bow on back of dress. Tie ribbon on wrist to secure sprinkling can, and put daisy in hand. Place flowers in grass. Attach stars with dots of icing. Serves 20.

TORCH OF LIBERTY
shown on page 87

First make torch using Color Flow technique and CELEBRATE II pattern. Outline with tube 2 and flow in icing, making the flames and criss-cross areas extra thick and puffy. Make stars separately; outline with tube 1 and flow in.

Bake and ice a Long Loaf cake. Pipe tube 12 puff border around bottom of cake; trim with tube 16 stars and tube 2 blue stringwork. Pipe tube 16 shell border around top edge of cake. Pipe mounds of icing as base for torch and position on cake. Add stars with dots of icing and set flags at base. Serves 16.

HAPPY BIRTHDAY, AMERICA!
shown on page 86

Bake a birthday cake for our country's celebration!

First prepare shield, stars and oval, using patterns and Color Flow technique. When oval is dry, pipe lettering with tube 2 and edge with tube 4 beading. Pipe olive brances on wax paper with tube 15, add tube 4 olives and dry.

Figure-pipe eagle on wax paper taped over pattern. Outline lower part of wings with tube 101s, then move upward, filling in space to top of wing. Pipe top arch of wing with tube 6; fill in wing feathers and tail feathers with tube 101s. Next pipe tube 6 breast area, and overpipe with tube 101s feathers. With tube 6, pipe neck, head, feet and claws.

Bake and ice a two-layer 12" x 4" cake and a two-layer oval cake. Pipe a tube 22 shell border at base and top of square cake and at base of oval cake. Pipe tube 15 zigzag drapes on sides of oval cake. Attach branches with dots of icing, then pipe a tube 3 "rope". Attach lettered oval, set branches at sides and pipe another tube 3 "rope" to join branches. Pipe tube 2 lettering on top of square cake.

Position eagle on oval cake, propping with mound of icing. Pipe a tube 44 ribbon across eagle and trim with tube 225 stars. Set shield in place. Serves 48.

IN HONOR OF OUR FIRST PRESIDENT
shown on page 87

First do all Color Flow pieces for top of cake, using CELEBRATE II pattern. Make all leaves separately in two shades of green, and dry on Flower Formers. When dry, add center veins in contrasting green with tube 1. Next do hatchet, bow-and-streamers (made in two sections) and stem, flowing in icing for a puffy effect. Make white stars for streamers separately and attach with icing when dry. Flow in knot of bow on hatchet, after hatchet dries. Also in advance, make marzipan cherries using recipe on page 96. Mount some on wires to go around edge of cake.

Now bake and ice a 12" x 4" round cake. Pipe tube 2 lettering on side. Pipe tube 21 puff border around base and top of cake. On bottom border, drop tube 2 strings and pipe a tiny knot between each pair of puffs. Pipe tube 65 leaves between each pair of puffs on top edge of cake. Bend wires on the mounted cherries and insert them in top edge.

Assemble the Color Flow pieces, using pattern as a guide. Raise all pieces on piped mounds of icing for dimensional effect. First place most of the leaves, then the stem, bow-and-streamers and finally hatchet. Finish with more leaves and cherries. Serves 22.

EVERYBODY LOVES IT!

CELEBRATE! II'S CHOICE in the monthly recipe contests! From hundreds of truly distinguished recipes the CELEBRATE! II panel has—with difficulty—chosen these. Congratulations to the winners and most sincere thanks to all. These are certain to be gratefully received by all.

MARCH RECIPE WINNERS

Marjorie McDonald, Panorama City, California, shares the recipe for this marvelous Chicken Casserole with CELEBRATE! II readers. "Fantastic", "excellent", "great combination of flavors" are just a few of the comments our tasters gave after sampling this casserole.

CHICKEN CASSEROLE

Pastry:
   2 cups all-purpose flour
   ¼ teaspoon salt
   ¾ cup butter, softened
   1 package (8 ounces) cream cheese

Filling:
   2 packages (10 ounces each) frozen broccoli spears
   1 can (6 or 8 ounces) water chestnuts, drained and sliced
   3 cups cubed cooked chicken
   1 can (10½ ounces) condensed cream of chicken soup
   1 can (10½ ounces) condensed cream of celery soup
   1 cup dairy sour cream
   1 teaspoon Worcestershire sauce
   ½ teaspoon curry powder
   ⅛ teaspoon ground nutmeg
   1 cup shredded sharp Cheddar cheese

1. For pastry, mix flour and salt. Blend butter and cream cheese, add flour, and mix with a pastry blender. Refrigerate a fourth of dough. Press remaining dough onto bottom and sides of a greased 13x9-inch baking dish (3 quart).

2. For filling, cook broccoli, following package directions, until crisp-tender; drain and put onto dough in baking dish. Put water chestnuts, then chicken on top.

3. Combine soups, sour cream, Worcestershire sauce, curry powder, and nutmeg. Spoon over chicken. Sprinkle with cheese.

4. Bake at 375°F 20 minutes.

5. Meanwhile, roll out remaining dough on a lightly floured surface to ¼-inch thickness; cut into strips.

6. Arrange pastry strips in a lattice design on top of casserole mixture. Bake 20 minutes. 6 to 8 servings. Freezes well.

Becky Westfield of Bowie, Maryland sends this recipe for a "breakfast that tastes as good as apple pie". It would serve just as well as dessert for luncheon or supper. Becky is just 14, which proves that good cooks start young.

BREAKFAST CASSEROLE

   5 or 6 apples (about 2 pounds)
   1 tablespoon lemon juice
   ¼ cup butter or margarine
   2½ cups corn flakes
   ½ cup brown sugar
   1 teaspoon ground cinnamon
   ½ cup apple juice, heated

1. Pare and slice apples; put into a bowl, drizzle with lemon juice, and toss to coat.

2. Melt butter in a skillet; add corn flakes and coat with butter. Divide into 3 portions.

3. Spoon 1 portion of flakes into a 1½-quart casserole. Spoon in half the apple slices. Mix brown sugar and cinnamon; sprinkle half over apples. Repeat layering, ending with corn flakes. Pour hot apple juice over all. Cover casserole.

4. Bake at 350°F 10 minutes. Remove cover and bake 40 minutes. 6 to 8 servings.

Ann Broda of Collinsville, Illinois submitted this recipe for Czechoslovakian Sugar Horns. Mrs. Broda makes these for Christmas, but they are so crisp and light and flavorful, you won't want to save them just for the holidays. She writes, "These cookies freeze well, and when thawed are just as crisp as when freshly baked".

CZECHOSLOVAKIAN SUGAR HORNS

Dough:
   ½ pint dairy sour cream
   1 package active dry yeast
   5 cups all-purpose flour
   1 pound margarine, softened
   1 egg
   3 egg yolks
   Lemon juice or grated lemon peel

Nut filling:
   3 cups ground nuts
   2 cups sugar
   ½ teaspoon ground cinnamon
   1 teaspoon vanilla extract
   Milk

1. For dough, warm sour cream, sprinkle yeast over it, and stir until yeast is dissolved. Add flour, margarine, egg, yolks, and a small amount of lemon juice or grated peel; mix well. Cover and refrigerate overnight.

2. For filling, mix nuts, sugar, cinnamon, vanilla extract, and enough milk to make a thick paste.

3. Roll out a fourth of pastry at a time to ⅛-inch thickness on a lightly floured surface. Cut into 3-inch squares. Take each square and roll out on a surface sprinkled with granulated sugar into a little larger square. Put about 1 teaspoon filling onto a corner of each square, roll jelly-roll fashion, and shape into crescents. Put on greased cookie sheets.

4. Bake at 350°F about 20 minutes, or until lightly browned. Makes 6½ dozen.

APRIL RECIPE WINNERS

Betty Morton of Tulsa, Oklahoma, sends this recipe for a marvelous, quick-to-make hot hors d'oeuvre. She makes a triple batch early in December, freezes them and then takes them out as she needs them for holiday parties. She makes the sauce in a fondue pot or electric skillet, then adds the meat balls and heats till piping hot.

SWEET AND SOUR MEATBALLS

   1 pound ground beef
   ½ cup dry bread crumbs

⅓ cup minced onion
¼ cup milk
1 egg
1 tablespoon chopped parsley
1 teaspoon salt
⅛ teaspoon pepper
½ teaspoon Worcestershire sauce
¼ cup shortening
1 bottle (12 ounces) chili sauce
1 jar (10 ounces) grape jelly

1. Combine ground beef, crumbs, onion, milk, egg, and seasonings in a bowl; mix lightly. Gently shape into 1-inch balls.

2. Melt shortening in a large skillet. Add meatballs and brown on all sides. Remove meatballs from skillet and pour off fat.

3. Put chili sauce and jelly into skillet and heat, stirring constantly, until jelly is melted. Add meatballs and stir until coated. Simmer 30 minutes. About 40.

Mrs. Ralph A. Labinski of Menomonee Falls, Wisconsin, shares this luscious Date-Nut Bread with us. Delicious plain or spread with butter or cream cheese. Mrs. Labinski has frozen the bread for as long as six months.

DATE NUT ROLL

2 cups (1 pound) pitted dates, chopped
4 teaspoons baking soda
4 cups boiling water
8 cups all-purpose flour
1 teaspoon salt
2 cups sugar
2 cups light or dark brown sugar
½ pound butter or margarine, melted
4 eggs
2 cups ground walnuts or pecans
4 teaspoons vanilla extract

1. Put dates into a large bowl, sprinkle baking soda over them, and pour boiling water over all. Set aside to cool.

2. Mix flour and salt.

3. Put sugars and butter into a large mixer bowl; mix well. Add eggs, one at a time, beating well after each addition. Add dry ingredients and date mixture alternately to creamed mixture, mixing well after each addition. Add nuts and vanilla; mix well.

4. Fill greased containers about half full with batter. Use sixteen Wilton Little Loafers, thirteen 16- or 17- ounce fruit cans or 7x4-inch loaf pans, six 1-pound coffee cans, or a combination.

5. Bake at 350°F about 1 hour to 1 hour and 15 minutes, or until a cake tester comes out clean. Remove from oven and cool in containers on wire racks. 6 to 16 loaves depending on size. Note: The cooled loaves can be wrapped tightly in foil and stored in a freezer for about 6 months.

MAY RECIPE WINNERS

Mrs. Holger Gram of Kimball, Nebraska, sends this recipe for the best Whole Wheat Bread we've ever tasted! The Grams raise and grind their own wheat, but even using the "store-bought" variety gives spectacular results.

WHOLE WHEAT-COTTAGE CHEESE BREAD

3¾ cups whole wheat flour (or half whole wheat and half all-purpose flour)
2 packages active dry yeast
½ teaspoon baking soda
1½ cups creamed cottage cheese
½ cup water
2 tablespoons margarine
¼ cup packed dark brown sugar
2 teaspoons salt
2 eggs

1. Mix 1½ cups flour, undissolved yeast, and baking soda in a large bowl.

2. Combine cottage cheese, water, margarine, brown sugar, and salt in a saucepan. Heat until just warm, stirring to melt margarine. Add warmed mixture to dry ingredients, then add eggs and beat at low speed until blended, about ½ minute. Beat at high speed 3 minutes. Stir in enough more flour to make a stiff dough.

3. Knead dough on a floured surface 8 to 10 minutes. Put dough into a greased bowl; cover and let rise in a warm place until double in bulk, about 1 hour.

4. Punch dough down and shape into about 2½ dozen rolls and put into two greased 9-inch round pans or shape into 2 loaves and put into greased 8¼x4½x2½-inch loaf pans. Let rise until double in bulk.

5. Bake at 375°F about 20 minutes for rolls and about 25 minutes for bread. About 2½ dozen rolls or 2 loaves bread.

Edna Andrues of San Jose, California, sends a Chocolate Sponge Cake recipe she received from her mother when she was a teenager. The cake has a subtle, unusual flavor, and the frosting is a delight!

CHOCOLATE SPONGE CAKE

1¼ cups plus 1 tablespoon sifted cake flour
3 tablespoons ground semi-sweet chocolate
6 large egg yolks
6 tablespoons cold water
1 teaspoon vanilla extract
½ teaspoon salt
1 cup sugar

6 egg whites
½ cup sugar
Frosting (see recipe)

1. Mix cake flour and chocolate.

2. Beat egg yolks, water, vanilla extract, and salt until frothy. Add 1 cup sugar gradually, beating until *very thick* and light in color. Fold in flour mixture.

3. Beat egg whites until frothy. Add ½ cup sugar gradually, beating until soft peaks are formed. Fold meringue carefully into egg yolk mixture. Pour carefully into an ungreased 10-inch tube pan. Cut through batter with a knife.

4. Bake at 350°F 45 to 50 minutes.

5. Invert to cool. Remove cake from pan and frost. One 10-inch tube cake.

Frosting

Beat 1 large egg; add 6 tablespoons margarine. Add sifted powdered sugar (about 3½ cups) until frosting is of spreading consistency. Melt 2 ounces (2 squares) unsweetened chocolate with 1 teaspoon margarine. Spoon melted chocolate over cake and let drip down sides.

Judy Bottasso of Eielson Air Force Base shares a Philippine recipe given her by a friend. She always uses it for special dinners when she wants to impress friends— and the guests always rave!

PHILIPPINE CHICKEN CASSEROLE
(Manok sa Casserole)

3 large chicken breasts, cut in half
½ teaspoon salt
¼ teaspoon pepper
¼ cup butter or margarine
1 can (10½ ounces) condensed cream of chicken soup
½ cup sauterne
1 can (6 or 8 ounces) water chestnuts, drained and sliced paper thin
1 can (3 ounces) broiled sliced mushrooms
¼ cup chopped green pepper
¼ teaspoon crushed thyme

1. Season chicken with salt and pepper.

2. Heat butter in a large skillet, add chicken, and brown slowly.

3. Arrange chicken, skin side up, in an 8x12-inch baking dish (2-quart).

4. Discard fat in skillet. Add soup to skillet while stirring. Add wine and stir until smooth. Add water chestnuts, mushrooms, green pepper, and thyme; mix well. Bring to boiling. Pour sauce over chicken. Cover baking dish with aluminum foil.

5. Bake at 350°F 25 minutes. Uncover and continue baking 25 to 35 minutes, or until chicken is tender.

6. Serve over hot fluffy rice. 6 servings.

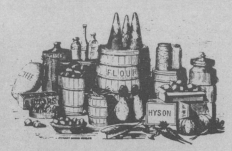

JUNE RECIPE WINNERS

Mary Witt of Mesquite, Texas, provides a recipe for savory Cheese Balls that's easy to prepare, no trouble to store and, served with crisp crackers or celery, "is a perfect snack or a before-dinner appetizer".

CHEESE BALLS

    1 carton (8 ounces) pimento cheese
       spread
    1 package (8 ounces) sharp cheddar
       cheese, grated
    2 packages (3 ounces each) cream
       cheese
    Dash Worcestershire sauce
    3 tablespoons grated onion
    ½ teaspoon grated garlic
    Mayonnaise
    Parsley flakes

1. Beat cheeses, Worcestershire sauce, onion, and garlic. Add desired amount of mayonnaise. Chill until easy to handle.
2. Shape into balls, roll in parsley flakes, and refrigerate.

Mrs. Jerome Donnelly of Terre Haute, Indiana, offers this Carrot Cake recipe. When a voice vote was given by the members of the test panel, the hurrahs were loud and sincere.

CARROT CAKE

    4 eggs
    1½ cups cooking oil
    2 cups grated carrots
    2 cups sifted all-purpose flour
    2 cups sugar
    1 teaspoon baking soda
    1 teaspoon salt
    1 teaspoon cinnamon
    Frosting

1. Mix eggs, oil, and carrots.
2. Blend flour, sugar, baking soda, salt, and cinnamon thoroughly. Add to carrot mixture and mix well.
3. Turn into a greased and floured 9 x 13-inch sheet cake pan.
4. Bake at 350°F 50 to 60 minutes, or until done. Cool on a wire rack. Frost; refrigerate until ready to serve.
Frosting:
    ½ cup (1 stick) butter
    1 package (8 ounces) cream cheese
    1 box (1 pound) confectioners' sugar
    2 teaspoons vanilla extract
    Pinch salt
    1 cup chopped pecans
    1 small can crushed pineapple,
       drained
Cream butter and cheese well. Mix in remaining ingredients.

From **Mrs. Arthur Werner** comes a recipe for Melt-aways, sugar cookies that couldn't be more aptly named! If you have come around to the notion that the humble sugar cookie is somewhat of a humdrum shortbread, the neatly-formed Melt-aways may very well change your mind.

MELT-AWAYS (SUGAR COOKIES)

    1 cup butter
    1 cup vegetable oil
    1 cup granulated sugar
    1 cup powdered sugar
    1 teaspoon vanilla extract
    2 eggs
    4 cups all-purpose flour
    1 teaspoon baking soda
    1 teaspoon cream of tartar
    1 teaspoon salt

1. Combine butter, oil, sugars, and vanilla extract in a large bowl. Beat until thoroughly creamed. Add eggs and beat well.
2. Sift flour, baking soda, cream of tartar, and salt together; add to creamed mixture and mix well.
3. Chill at least 2 hours.
4. Shape dough into small balls, roll in sugar and place on lightly greased cookie sheets. Press with glass dipped in sugar.
5. Bake at 375°F 12 minutes. About 8 dozen cookies.

JULY RECIPE WINNERS

Mrs. Joseph Degi, Jr. of Fort Stewart, Georgia, shares one of her compliment-winning recipes—Turkey Stroganoff. It's an ideal, and rather elegant, main dish for a buffet dinner, and Sylvia Degi reports that it freezes well for up to a month.

TURKEY STROGANOFF

    ½ cup chopped green pepper
    ¼ cup chopped onion
    ¼ cup butter or margarine
    2 cans (about 10 ounces each)
       condensed cream of
       mushroom soup
    1½ cups dairy sour cream
    1 teaspoon salt
    10 ounces broad noodles, cooked
    3 cups diced cooked turkey
    1 teaspoon paprika

1. Cook green pepper and onion in butter until tender.
2. Blend soup, sour cream, and salt. Add onion, green pepper, cooked noodles, and turkey; mix well. Turn into a greased 13 x 9-inch baking pan. Sprinkle with paprika.
3. Bake at 350°F 30 minutes, or until bubbly. 10 to 12 servings.

Mrs. Daniel Pritchard of Spalding, Nebraska, gives those CELEBRATE! readers who believe the dessert is the high point of the

meal a recipe that can do nothing but back up their opinion! Her Strawberry Cream Roll is certain to delight anyone who considers nothing can match a plump, ripe strawberry—particularly when it's embellished by fine-textured cake and a generous touch of whipped cream.

STRAWBERRY CREAM ROLL

    1 cup sifted all-purpose flour
    2 teaspoons baking powder
    ½ teaspoon salt
    10 egg yolks
    1 cup sugar
    ½ cup water
    1 teaspoon lemon extract
    Confectioners' sugar
    1 pint sliced strawberries
    ½ pint whipped cream

1. Sift flour, baking powder, and salt together.
2. Beat egg yolks, sugar, water, and lemon extract until thick and lemon-colored (about 5 minutes). Fold in dry ingredients.
3. Spread batter in waxed paper lined 15½ x 10½ x 1-inch jelly-roll pan.
4. Bake at 400°F about 20 minutes, or until done. Loosen cake around edges. Turn out onto dish towel dusted with confectioners' sugar. Roll up as for jelly roll. Cool completely.
5. Unroll cake and spread with a mixture of strawberries and whipped cream to within ½ inch of edges. Reroll cake. Place open end down. Refrigerate until serving time.
6. Serve topped with whipped cream and strawberries. 12 servings.

June Kelley of Davie, Florida, offers the recipe she likes best for the Doctor Bird Cake which she says is "often used in Florida instead of the traditional fruit cake for the Christmas holidays".

According to June, the doctor—a Fort Lauderdale pioneer—worked up this basic recipe using fruits native to that area. June says it "seem to be a special favorite with those who do not like very rich desserts. For best flavor, do not cut for 12 hours after baking".

DOCTOR BIRD CAKE

    3 cups all-purpose flour
    2 cups sugar
    1 teaspoon cinnamon
    1 teaspoon baking soda
    1 teaspoon salt
    1½ cups peanut oil
    3 eggs, well beaten
    1½ teaspoons vanilla extract
    ¼ teaspoon almond extract
    2 bananas, peeled and diced
    1 can (8¼ ounces) crushed
       pineapple; undrained

1. Mix flour, sugar, cinnamon, baking soda, and salt in a large bowl. Add remaining ingredients and mix.
2. Turn batter into a greased and floured 9-inch tube or Bundt pan.
3. Baked at 350°F about 1 hour and 10 minutes, or until cake tests done. One 9-inch tube cake.

AUGUST RECIPE WINNERS

Jean Osborn of Benicia, California gives us a recipe for Piccadilly Pudding that has been a source of delight to dinner guests of the Osborn family for the past thirty years! Jean indicates "it can be made ahead and frozen for a short time but the peanut brittle has a tendency to get wet if frozen too long."

PICCADILLY PUDDING
    1½ cups sugar
    ½ cup water
    8 egg whites
    6 egg yolks, well beaten
    1 tablespoon lemon juice
    1 cup sifted cake flour
    ¾ teaspoon cream of tartar
    3 cups Custard Filling
    1 cup finely crushed peanut
       brittle
    1½ cups whipping cream
    ¼ cup powdered sugar
    1½ cups flaked coconut
    ½ teaspoon almond extract

1. Combine 1½ cups sugar and the water in small, heavy saucepan. Boil to 240°F (about 5 min. after rapid boiling starts).
2. Meanwhile, beat egg whites until stiff, not dry, peaks are formed.
3. Pour syrup slowly in a fine stream onto beaten egg whites, beating until cool (about 10 minutes). Add beaten egg yolks and lemon juice and fold together.
4. Sift flour three times with cream of tartar; gently fold into egg mixture.
5. Turn into a 10-inch tube pan.
6. Bake at 350°F 45 to 50 minutes.
7. Take from oven and invert pan until cake is cool before removing from pan.
8. Cut cake into 4 even layers. Enlarge center hole in top three layers, leaving a 2-inch wall of cake. Fill hole in bottom layer with extra cake, making a solid layer.
9. To 1½ cups of custard filling, add and mix in peanut brittle. Spread some of it evenly over bottom layer and place next layer on top.
10. Whip cream until stiff; mix in powdered sugar and coconut. Spread second layer with coconut cream and top with next layer. Spread with remaining peanut brittle custard. Cover with top layer of cake.
11. Crumble remaining extra cake and mix along with almond extract into remaining custard. Fill center hole of cake. Frost top and sides with remaining coconut cream. Chill several hours before cutting. 12 servings.

Custard Filling:
    ½ cup sifted cake flour
    1 cup sugar
    ½ teaspoon salt
    2 eggs, slightly beaten
    2½ cups milk, scalded
    1 teaspoon vanilla extract
1. Mix flour, sugar, and salt in a heavy saucepan. Stir in beaten eggs. Pour in scalded milk gradually, mixing well. Bring to boil, stirring constantly, cook 4 minutes.
2. Remove from heat and add vanilla extract. Cool before using. About 3 cups.

Helen Wooldridge has generously passed along a recipe for Best Ever Applesauce Fruitcake given to her by her mother-in-law, **Mrs. Hulda Wooldridge** of Las Cruces, New Mexico. In addition to being both unique and delicious, Helen Wooldridge says the cake "keeps well for about two months or more when tightly wrapped— also freezes well".

BEST-EVER APPLESAUCE FRUITCAKE
    3 cups all-purpose flour
    2 teaspoons baking soda
    1 teaspoon baking powder
    ½ teaspoon cloves
    ½ teaspoon nutmeg
    ½ teaspoon cinnamon
    ½ teaspoon salt
    1 pound candied cherries
    ½ pound mixed candied fruit
    1 jar (8 ounces) candied pineapple
    ¾ cup dates
    1 cup raisins
    1½ cups pecans
    1½ cups walnuts
    ½ cup butter
    1 cup sugar
    2 eggs
    ½ cup grape juice
    1½ cups applesauce
1. Sift and mix flour, baking soda, baking powder, spices, and salt.
2. Cut up fruit and coarsely chop nuts. Mix fruit and nuts.
3. Cream butter and sugar. Add eggs and beat well.
4. Beating until blended after each addition, alternately add dry ingredients and grape juice to creamed mixture. Mix in fruit, nuts, and applesauce.
5. Turn into a greased 10-inch tube pan.
6. Bake at 275°F about 2½ hours.
7. Run a knife around tube and sides and let set about 10 minutes in pan. Remove cake and cool thoroughly. Keeps well for about 2 months or more when tightly wrapped; it also freezes well. Yields one 6-pound fruitcake.

Mrs. Lois Kuhns of Cleveland Heights, Ohio, offers an impressive Hawaiian Party Cake recipe for the dessert fancier who is willing to spend extra time and energy for a cake that's truly distinguished.

HAWAIIAN PARTY CAKE
    3¼ cups sifted cake flour
    2 cups sugar
    4½ teaspoons baking powder
    1½ teaspoons salt
    ¾ cup shortening
    1½ cups milk
    1 teaspoon vanilla extract
    ½ teaspoon lemon extract
    ½ teaspoon orange extract
    2 egg whites
    3 egg yokes
    ¼ cup drained crushed pineapple
    1 tablespoon grated orange peel
    Few drops yellow food coloring
    Pineapple pudding frosting
    Orange filling
    Flaked coconut
1. Combine flour, sugar, baking powder, and salt in a bowl. Add shortening, milk, and extracts. Beat 2 minutes at medium speed with mixer.
2. Measure 1½ cups batter into a second bowl and add egg whites. Beat 2 minutes at medium speed on mixer. Pour into a waxed-paper-lined 9-inch layer cake pan.
3. Add yolks, pineapple, grated peel, and food coloring, if desired, to remaining batter. Beat 2 minutes on medium speed. Pour into 2 waxed-paper-lined round layer cake pans.
4. Bake layers at 350°F 25 to 30 minutes.
5. Cool cake layers.
6. Starting with a yellow layer, spread with a thin layer of frosting and half of filling; top with white layer and continue layering. Frost top and sides. Sprinkle with additional coconut. One 3-layer, 9-inch cake.
Pineapple Pudding Frosting:
    ½ cup butter
    ½ cup shortening
    1 cup confectioners' sugar
    ½ teaspoon vanilla extract
    1 teaspoon orange extract
    1 package (3¾ ounces) instant
       pineapple cream pudding
    ½ cup milk
    ½ cup coffee cream or half-and-half
1. Combine butter, shortening, sugar, and extracts in a bowl; beat until creamy, about 10 minutes.
2. In small bowl, empty contents of pudding package; add milk and cream, mix, and let set about 5 minutes. Combine the mixtures and beat 10 minutes until light and fluffy. About 2¼ cups frosting.

Chris Watson, Richmond, Va. tells how she solved the problem of a Panda cake with a broken-off head. "I trimmed the back off the head so it would lie flat and positioned a heart cake below it. Then I trimmed the feet and put them at the bottom of the heart. For the forepaws, I trimmed curved pieces of cake so the paws curved over the heart as if the Panda were holding it. What started out as a disaster ended up a success!"

Barbara J. Berquist, Rickenbacker AFB, Ohio writes: "Fill a tall Pepsi bottle with water and decorate Mr. Panda on it. The tube that stays inside the cake fits well and won't fall over." She adds, "Your offset coupler is a must for decorating shaped cakes . . . under chins, ears and feet."

Laura Budd of Galena, Ohio writes: "I use an electric knife to do all my trimming; it cuts so smooth on a warm or cold cake."

Another baking tip comes from **Linda Cope** of Delphi, Ind. She writes: "I use mixes but add 1 envelope whipped topping mix, 4 eggs and 1 cup of water to each mix. For white cakes, I use 5 egg whites instead of 4 eggs. They are always moist and don't crumble. I also wrap wet towels around my pans so they bake evenly and without a hump."

NEW IDEAS—NEW PRODUCTS

Judy Bottasso, Eielson Air Force Base, APO Seattle, shares a discovery. "I've used drop flower tubes for making 'shell' borders. Not all the tubes can be used this way, but the ones that make really great borders are 1F, 1G, 2D and 2F. They're especially good on large sheet cakes."

Another time-saver comes from **Kitty Terrell,** Charlotte, N.C. "I set up a loose-leaf notebook of visual ideas. This included decorations I liked from CELEBRATE!, from your catalog, magazines and newspapers. It makes decorating ideas easier to find."

Janet L. Anderson of North East, Md. suggests: "Please come out with a motorcycle novelty. I have a lot of requests for them. I'd also like emblems for 10th, 15th, 20th, 30th, 35th and 40th anniversaries."

Mary Forrester of Sturgies, S.D. would like "a basic set of lesson plans for those intending to teach cake decorating."

Thank you for your suggestions. They are being studied at this time.

Many readers have asked for charts showing cake-cutting methods and amounts of batter needed for various-sized pans. Please consult page 158.

Mrs. Leroy McCann, Oxford, Ohio asks if Wilton could make available bill books and order books. She continues, "I would like to see lots of new wedding cake designs."

THANKS for WRITING

Advice and Adventures from our decorating readers

We hope Mrs. McCann will like the wedding cakes in this book, in The Wilton Way of Cake Decorating and in our 1976 YEAR-BOOK. Standard invoice forms may be purchased at stationery stores or small local printers.

Color Flow brings forth much comment from our readers. **Mrs. Truman B. Gibson** of Trona, Cal. writes "I enjoy your Color Flow patterns. I use them by cutting out the pattern from wax paper, tracing it on the icing, then outline with slightly thickened frosting, and fill in with icing thinned down a little. I use a small paint brush to spread it out." She adds, "Wish you'd make rubber molds instead of plastic; they are much easier to pop out."

Please see page 176 in the 1976 YEAR-BOOK for new synthetic rubber molds.

Esther Nebenfuhr of Garden Grove, Cal. writes, "I just discovered a great little trick. Instead of taping the waxed paper to Color Flow patterns, use 3M's new Pinless Pattern Holder. The waxed paper can be repositioned and it is held smooth against the pattern with no slipping and is easy to move afterwards."

Here's an appealing way to use pieces trimmed off a round cake in leveling, from **Louise T. Deshaies,** Greensboro, N. C. "The leveled off part is round (top of each layer); cut this into two pieces. Place the cut edges side by side on platter holding together with icing, rounded edges to outside. The side view looks like a half circle, which immediately suggests certain shapes: mouse, fish, bunny are the ones I have done." She adds cardboard ears, fins, makes eyes with jelly beans or icing and

pipes mouth and tail. She asks, "Which is the best kind of camera to take a clear close-up picture of a cake?"

Our photographer suggests a Kodak Instamatic for non-professional photographers. Other tips: take the picture outside, before 10:30 a.m. or from 2:00 p.m. till sundown. Keep backgrounds simple.

Speaking of photos, **Alice Garcia,** Oakdale, Cal. says, "To take a detailed picture, set the cake by a window. No flash cubes are necessary."

SUGGESTIONS FOR CELEBRATE! II

Mary Lou Thomson of Rexburg, Idaho, writes, "I would enjoy very much having more information about the colors used on your photographed cakes."

Please refer to Norman Wilton's "Commonsense" in this book.

Carolyn Peace of Arnold, Md. has two questions for us: "Can we have the same quality photos and directions for making and decorating hors d'oeuvres as we have had for cakes in CELEBRATE! II? I'd also love candy recipes."

So many readers have informed us that their main interest is in decorating cakes that we have concentrated on this subject in CELEBRATE! II. There are many good cookbooks that give information on hors d'oeuvres, including the Pillsbury Family Cookbook. Please see our holiday candy article on page 131 in this book.

Marianne Lopriore of Grafton, Mass. asks: "Could you have some cake ideas for boys' birthdays?"

We've included cakes for boys in CELEBRATE! II. There is also a special group of boys' cakes in the 1976 Wilton YEARBOOK.

From Southington, Conn., **Mary R. Sheehan** writes: "How will I be able to enjoy the patterns on upcoming holiday cakes if CELEBRATE! comes out once a year?"

All patterns for CELEBRATE! II are published in the CELEBRATE! II Pattern Book, as well as patterns from the 1976 YEAR-BOOK and all 1974 issues of CELEBRATE! This should be an advantage as all patterns are together to use anytime.

TIPS FOR DECORATING

Dorothy Ramsay of Tualatin, Ore., sent us a hint. "I would like to share what I think is an original idea. I fill a large writing tube with green, insert a toothpick in the hole, and squeeze the bag as I pull it out, making my stem. To make roses I put a dot of green icing on the end of the stem and use it like a flower nail." Dorothy makes a hollyhock type flower with a similar technique.

Continued on next page

From **Miriam H. Hilsher,** Elizabethtown, Pa. "I use one box of Pillsbury Cake Mix and one recipe of my own homemade yellow cake, combined, and fold the two together. My cakes have the lightness of the mix and the good flavor of my own."

Nadine Horning of Calgary, Alberta advises, "Wilton cake pans make wonderful molds for gelatin salads."

And **Delores Prinkey** of Mt. Pleasant, Pa. offers a money-making idea: "I decorate cupcakes for schools and banquets. I put a big flower and leaf on top of each iced cupcake. I also make up flowers separately for people to do with as they wish. I sell three dozen flowers for $1.00."

Cathryn Hix of Fresno, Cal. tells how she turns an ice cream cone into a cornucopia. "I saw it in three pieces with a coping saw and then glue the pieces together with royal icing to form the curve of the cornucopia. When dry, decorate."

TRANSFERRING CAKE LAYERS

Several readers offered solutions for the problem of transferring large cake layers. **Jean Bergman** of Sand Lake, Mich. writes, "Freeze your cakes in the pan. When removing the cake from the freezer, turn it bottom side up and run hot water over the pan. The cake slides out and is very easy to handle. It does not break and the pans need no more than a light greasing. I also line the bottom of the pan with wax paper. Be sure the cake is thoroughly cooled before freezing."

Another tip is from **Mrs. Arthur Wendel** of New Weston, Pa. "I use a 12" support plate or cardboard and place it to one side of the 16" layer and turn bottom side up. This lets about 4" hang over. I slide the layer off the board and into place on the bottom layer. With icing partly dry it can be moved if need be."

Mrs. Daniel Pritchard, Spalding, Neb. writes, "I bake my large cake first, then freeze it while I bake my other cakes. When I am ready to ice my cakes the large one will be frozen and can be placed with no cracking. Let thaw, then ice."

Another idea comes from **Helen Stenzel** of Osco, Ill. "Place a large cake circle over the layer, covering the circle first with wax paper. Place it in the freezer till nearly frozen. Ice the bottom layer filling and put the frozen cake on top. It will soon thaw. Work with it then; no breakage."

Mrs. M. Schultz of Fishkill, N.Y. suggests using 2 spatulas or a large cookie sheet. She says, "I transfer large layers and find them easy to handle by using a large cookie sheet without edges and sliding the cake off the sheet onto the bottom layer. Filling is not disturbed and the layer does not crack or break.

Norman Wilton gives this advice. "To move a large cake layer from rack, place wax paper covered cardboard on top of cake, flip over and place second cardboard on bottom. Flip over again and slide off."

DECORATING QUESTIONS AND ANSWERS

Norine Braden of Wayne, Mich. inquires, "Could you please tell me how to get scallops on cakes even?"

See The Wilton Way of Cake Decorating, Chapter Seven, on making patterns.

From **Mrs. Prontkowski** of Fowlerville, Mich., this question: "How much meringue powder to use in a 9" meringue pie?"

Meringue powder is not intended for this use, only for icing. Fresh egg white will give better flavor and texture for pie.

Mrs. Steve J. Machart, Shiner, Tex., requests, "More pictures of square and rectangular sheet cakes and ideas for writing words on cakes such as Happy Birthday. Mrs. Machart also comments, "Some of the ingredients for candies and gum paste are hard to find".

A Color Flow question comes from **Mrs. A. J. Parks, Jr.** of Salinas, Cal. "Your Color Flow work is shiny, why isn't mine?"

Linda McCarty of Richmond, Va. writes, "Having such a hard time with Color Flow, I am wondering if there is any guideline to size of design and drying time."

Please see The Wilton Way of Cake Decorating, Chapter Fourteen, for a complete discussion of Color Flow. Cracks can often be mended from the back and touched

up. Be sure to dry under a heat lamp in humid weather.

Mrs. Max Redenius, Bradgate, Ia. "Your cake boards. What kind of colored foil do you use for your cake boards?"

We purchase the foil from a florist or florist supply shop. It is safe to use.

Icing colors concern **Mrs. Wayne Fitzgerald** of Cynthiana, Ky. "I hope you will have a chart on what colors mixed together will make what."

Please see "Commonsense" by Norman Wilton in this book.

COMMENTS AND STORIES

Many interesting stories are sent by CELEBRATE! readers such as **Mrs. H. A. Monger,** a former New Zealander now, living in Basingstoke, England. She writes, "As it was my father's 107th birthday I wondered how I should decorate for it. CELEBRATE! arrived; on the back cover was a cake decorated in a pretty shade of apricot. This year another CELEBRATE! gave me an idea for his 108th birthday!"

Congratulations to Mrs. Monger and may her father celebrate many more birthdays.

Another tribute comes from **Mrs. Clinton Gilmore,** Fair Oaks, Cal. "I want to say how much I have enjoyed CELEBRATE! Although it will be difficult waiting a year to receive the copies of CELEBRATE! II, I am glad they will be bound together in a hardback cover, since I refer to mine so frequently. They should be more durable."

A proud grandmother, **Mrs. John F. Dowell** of George West, Tex., sent a story about her 17-year-old granddaughter **Sue Dowell** and her cake decorating skills. Featured in the story was her masterpiece, a 3' x 5' replica of a local hotel, La Quinta Royale.

One of our busiest readers must be **Pat Tamulionis** of Security, Colo., who decorates and sells cakes, teaches decorating in her home and at a Women's Club in her home town, and has a husband and 4 daughters. She writes, "I also crochet, do needlepoint and other crafts, and sew for myself and four daughters, but nothing gives me enjoyment like creating a beautiful cake—I love cake decorating!"

Continued on next page

Kathy Hartig of Affton, Mo., who took up cake decorating about 5 years ago, writes: "With a new baby and a 3½ year old, no car and a husband who worked nights, I was pretty bored till I sent for the Wilton catalog". Now she teaches some classes in her home, demonstrates and does a steady business in cakes. She says, "I think I enjoy teaching almost more than selling. It's so rewarding to have a group of women who lack confidence in themselves, learn to do things they themselves can't believe!"

Faye Jones, Lufkin, Tex. writes, "I have been decorating about 4 years after ordering your YEARBOOK. I have not gone into business, but it seems there is always someone wanting me to make them a cake. Several women in our church became interested in cake decorating after a demonstration I gave at one of our monthly ladies' meetings."

A determined decorator is Lola K. Parker, Pilahatchie, Miss., who writes, "It started with your YEARBOOK and determination to try and do it. In February I signed up for an 8 week course, but a week before it started I was in a car wreck and so went through the 8 weeks with my left arm in a body sling. I am very proud of the cake which I made while I had the sling on. If I can decorate a cake while only using one arm, I can do anything!"

Sorry we haven't room to print the picture of a special blue-and-gold-trimmed 5th Anniversary cake Mrs. Donald Johnson of Wayne, Neb. baked for a local Senior Citizens Center. She tells us, "I bake cakes for my children and their friends' weddings, and mainly for the fun of seeing someone happy. I know the Senior Citizens are happy when they keep asking me to bake their cakes."

Marilyn McLain of St. Mary, Ohio, writes, "I have been decorating less than 4 years and do mostly birthday, holiday, and all-occasion cakes. I enjoy your books, CELEBRATE!, etc., but especially like to come up with a cake I've never seen or even seen a picture of before." She sent pictures of one of her originals, a cuckoo clock that won 1st place for Anniversary Cakes in a cake show.

So many readers mention learning decorating from the Wilton YEARBOOK, this should encourage Donna Reid of Pittsburgh, Pa., who writes that she has en-joyed looking through the YEARBOOK and wonders if she can learn to decorate with the Wilton film, since she cannot attend a course at present.

We would like to assure Donna that many have learned cake decorating from Wilton books and she can do it, too. Start by practicing techniques shown in the 1976 YEARBOOK, using the basic kit.

We often have inquiries about icing to use under conditions of high humidity, and a good answer from Hellen Smith, in Okinawa. She explains, "High humidity is something that we have in Okinawa. The following recipes are the best of several tried." She adds that the brands specified must be used and recommends mixing rather than whipping the icings. Hellen also states that "Only 2 of my Okinawan students speak any English but your pictures have made American and other types of cake decorating come alive for them."

HIGH HUMIDITY RECIPES

Okinawan Buttercream #1

  1½ cups Crisco
  ¼ cup dry Dream Whip
  ⅓ cup flour, non-sifted measure
    but sift before using
  2 pounds confectioners sugar
  ⅔ cup milk (less in very high
    humidity)

Combine Crisco and Dream Whip and mix well at slow speed. Then add, alternately, sifted flour, confectioners sugar and milk. Do not overmix, as this causes loss of texture.

Okinawan Buttercream #2

  1 cup Crisco
  ½ teaspoon salt
  1 teaspoon flavoring
  ½ cup milk
  3 tablespoons cornstarch
  2 pounds confectioners sugar, sifted

Combine Crisco, salt, flavoring, milk and mix well. Next add cornstarch and mix well, then add powdered sugar. Do not overmix. Cover bowl to prevent drying.

One of our most interesting letters came from Raquel Nobigrot of Mexico City. "I am a busy women, 28 years old, married to a pediatrician, mother of 3 children and love to entertain often." Raquel sent pictures and many interesting details of the decorations, cakes and other foods she prepared for her daughter Malkah's lavish 2nd birthday party, using the theme "Disney on Parade". She concludes, "Maybe one day I will have the opportunity to travel to your Wilton School and learn all the wonderful Wilton Course. This is my greatest desire!"

We hope your wish comes true!

READERS DISCOVER
MANY USES FOR
STORY BOOK DOLL PAN

The Story Book Doll Pan is the beginning of dozens of character cakes, as our readers have demonstrated. Here's a sampling:

Chris Farrin of Siloam Springs, Arkansas, gets a lot of use from her pan and sends the pictures to prove it! She writes, "We have some 90 people to bake birthday cakes for in our dining hall, about 75 of them kids. Clowns are most in demand for boys . . . I've made about a dozen of them over the last year and all different.

Some of her other creations are: Santa Claus in a bright red suit made with tube 48. A Toy Soldier with a cupcake "bearskin" hat, gold plume and gold trimming on his red coat and blue trousers. A Basketball Player in red shorts and shirt trimmed with white. He wears a big number "5" on his chest (the birthday boy's age) and white gym shoes.

And most surprisingly—a Rocket Ship! Chris trims the cake in a straight line from the "knob" on top of head to the hem of the dress. Some of the cake trimmings are used to make the three legs of the rocket and the entire cake is covered with white stars. Red and blue stripes are added, and the boy's name and age in large letters with tube 6. Our thanks and admiration to Chris Farrin for sharing her charming, imaginative cake ideas.

Rodelle Jorden of Memphis, Tennessee, bakes a freckled little boy in the Storybook Pan, wearing patched overalls and a red shirt. She trims the hair area and used the pieces to make a brim for his hat, trims off the arms and repositions them so that one

Continued on page 157

Decorate a Midwest barn, bulging
with the harvest of Autumn.
Directions, page 95

Autumn harvest

Cakes that express the joy of the season—photographed against glowing fall flowers.

AUTUMN HARVEST CAKE

First, make the basket. Using 5" mini-tier pans, bake two layers, fill and put together. Chill, then taper with sharp knife to about 3¾" at bottom. Then ice the cake. Make fruit and covering of marzipan (marzipan recipe on page 96).

To cover the basket, roll out marzipan and cut in ½" strips for sides. Cut narrower strips in red and green to circle basket, and attach to cake with royal icing. For wire handles, dye cloth-covered florists' wire copper color.

Next, make the fruits. Shape apples, grape clusters, corn and small pumpkins from tinted marzipan. For potatoes, use untinted marzipan; form into oval shape, make indentations with orangewood stick and roll in cocoa. For grapes, form small separate ovals and build up on pear-shaped base, working from bottom. Shape corn in a roll and score with knife; make corn husks from thinly rolled marzipan.

Now prepare the cake. Bake two 12" x 2" round layers, fill and ice. Pipe tube 10 ball border around base of cake; pipe tube 104 drape just above that and add tube 67 leaf at point of each drape. Pipe tube 2 vine and tube 67 leaves.

Arrange fruit basket on top of cake, placing fruits and vegetables as if spilling from it. Pipe leaves with tubes 65 and 68; add tube 7 brown stem to pumpkins and tube 1 tendrils to grapes. Serves 22.

Autumn glory

Decorating directions start on page 68

fun for children in the fall

AUTUMN DAYS are days of adventure for youngsters. To scuff through rustling fallen leaves on a crisp morning, to feel the stiffness of new fall outfits and to meet new friends at school—all say a new season is beginning. Make it even more fun with these bright, appeal-to-the-young cakes.

SCHOOL IS FUN! Take away the little fears and make the very first day a celebration with this cake for first grade scholars.

In advance, make tube 217 drop flowers. Mold book in sugar mold and, when firm, brush it with thinned royal icing. Pipe tube 3 lettering.

Next make cookie figures, using small Gingerbread boy and girl Cutters. After cookies have cooled, outline clothing with thinned Color Flow icing and tube 2. Then flow in color, making sure each color dries before adding next. Trim with tube 1 but-

tons, bows, hair, eyes, mouth and other little details.

Now bake, ice and assemble a 12"x 4" round cake, and an 8"x3" round. Pat top of 12" tier with damp sponge to achieve "grass" effect. Pipe a tube 21 star border around base of lower tier, and a tube 16 border around top and bottom of upper tier. Pipe lettering around 12" cake freehand or trace letters first with a toothpick. Set cookie figures around 8" tier with dots of icing. Set book on top of cake, propping with sugar cubes. Serves 30 little first graders.

GAMES ARE FUN! Even the youngest can be a winner in a family game of tic-tac-toe. Let the winner cut this cake as a just-before-bedtime treat.

Make the game symbols in Color Flow, using CELEBRATE! II patterns. Set aside to dry thoroughly.

Bake and ice a two-layer, 8" square cake. Make zigzag "X" design on sides, using tube 17. Edge base and top with tube 6 ball borders. Attach symbols to sides of cake with icing and set up the game on top. Serves 12 players (and spectators!).

HALLOWEEN IS LOTS OF FUN. Dressing up and trick-or-treating in the darkness. Coming home to a lively party with a scary Halloween cake!

Make the autumn leaves with softened Color Flow icing, just as described for Autumn Glory cake, page 69. Mold the pumpkins in sugar, using Heritage pumpkin mold. When dry, "paint" with thinned icing and pipe tube 199 stems.

The cakes are a 6" Ball cake and a 9"x 13" two-layer sheet cake. Set the sheet cake on a cake board and ice. Push in several dowels, even with its surface, to support ball cake. Ice the ball cake smoothly, then pipe grooves with tube 1A. Smooth grooves with a damp brush and pipe tube 4B stem. After icing has set, position on sheet cake, pushing dowel through to cake board to hold steady.

Now pipe a tube 506 shell border around base of sheet cake and trim with tube 2 dots. Set Scary Ghost figure on top, arrange small pumpkins and leaves and call everyone to the table. Serves 36 merry-makers.

PETER, PETER and his wife are happy with their pumpkin-shell home. Here's how to stage the scene.

Make windows and shutters using patterns and Color Flow technique. When dry, trim windows with tube 2 frames and tube 13 zigzag window boxes. Trim shutters with tube 2 hearts. Pipe drop flowers with tubes 13 and 225. Mount larger flowers on florist wire and pipe tube 65 leaves on wire, too.

Peter and his wife are shaped with large Gingerbread cutters. Before baking, insert toothpicks half way into feet to stick into cake later. After baking, outline with Color Flow icing and tube 1, then flow in areas. After drying, hair and features are piped with tube 2, cheeks with tube 4. Pipe Peter's pocket with tube 1 and trim apron with tube 3.

The "yard" is a 9" x 13" x 3" sheet cake. Ice smoothly, then pat top with a damp sponge. Pipe a base border of tube 363 pumpkins trimmed with tube 1 stems. Edge top with tube 19 rosettes.

The pumpkin house is baked in a 6" Ball pan, iced and assembled just as pumpkin cake described on page 109. Add tube 6 tendrils at top. Attach windows and shutters with icing and "plant" flowers in window boxes. Trim with tube 65s leaves.

Pipe tube 199 pumpkins around "house" with tube 4 stems. Set out wired flowers and fence the yard with a Colonial Fence. Put Peter and his wife in place. Serve to 36, with two lucky listeners claiming the cookies.

LITTLE BOY BLUE sleeps sweetly against a Wonder Mold cake haystack. He's shaped with the large Gingerbread cutter, too,

and decorated in the same manner as Peter and his wife, above. His collar and cuffs are piped with tube 102. His horn is figure piped with tube 7, then outlined with tube 1. Make drop flowers in advance with tubes 193 and 225.

Bake and ice a Wonder Mold cake. Put "hay" all over it with tube 233, starting at bottom and moving in random fashion to the top. Scatter drop flowers and attach Boy Blue to side with icing. Serves 12.

GOLDILOCKS and the Three Bears come to life on your table! Goldilocks is baked in a Blossom pan and uses a small doll pick. Papa and Mama are baked in the Panda pan and Baby Bear in the Panda Chocolate Mold. Before starting to decorate, make a recipe of gum paste (page 32) to use for aprons and buttons. Make tube 131 and tube 14 drop flowers.

Continued on page 72

TOUCH DOWN!

FOR THE HIGH SCHOOL SET

LIFE IS FULL FOR HIGH SCHOOLERS in the autumn, and sports and music are absorbing interest. Here are two very special sheet cakes to set the theme for teen get-togethers.

TOUCHDOWN! Cheer leaders jump for joy on an after-game cake.

Make their pompons in advance (directions start on page 90). Then bake and ice a two-layer 9" x 13" cake.

On top of the cake draw three stick figures with a toothpick—circle for head, stroke for body and lines for outstretched legs and arms. Pipe lines with tube 2. With tube 12, figure-pipe body, starting just above legs. Squeeze heavily, tapering to neck. Touch tube 10 to sides and base of body and use a steady, even pressure to squeeze out arms and legs. Touch same tube to top of neck and use even pressure

to fill in head. Repeat to make three figures. Pipe tube 6 shoes, with tube 13 zigzag for socks. Use tube 1 for shoelaces, hair, eyes and mouth. Make ruffle skirt with tube 124 and add tube 1 waistband.

Pipe tube 4 lettering along side of cake. Add borders with tube 21.

Secure pompons to ends of arms with icing and set clusters of pompons at each corner. Insert Football Picks. Serve to 24 sports enthusiasts.

A RECORD PARTY! Set out the coke and popcorn and, after they've listened for awhile, bring in this smashing record cake.

Pipe musical notes on wax paper and dry. Make pompons, or shaggy mums, in advance. (See page 90). Make 1¾" circles with Color Flow technique to use for record labels. When dry, add names of the guests' favorite pieces with tube 1.

Bake three round cakes in a set of Mini-tier pans and a 12" x 18" two-layer sheet cake. Ice the sheet cake smoothly. Ice sides of round cakes smoothly, tops thickly. Make grooves on tops with decorating comb and set labels in center. Edge with tube 1 beading. Now arrange "records" on top of sheet cake, propping one against the other.

Pipe five parallel, wavy lines on sides of sheet cake with tube 2 and attach musical notes with icing. Pipe tube 7 bulb borders at base and top of cake. Heap pompons on top of cake and finish with Teen Swinger figures. Serves 66 adults or 22 teen agers.

CONGRATULATIONS, YOU WON!

Entries for CELEBRATE! II's children's cake contest brought in a zoo's worth of adorable cake animals, an army of toy soldiers and a parade of beautiful dolls. Choosing winners wasn't easy, but here they are!

1st PRIZE: A BIRTHDAY DUCK

First prize and a gift certificate for $25 goes to **Norma Bailey** of Bethalto, Illinois. Her winning effort is a web-footed friend every child will adore! She fashioned him of 3 cakes: a Wonder Mold, an 8" round layer and a 12" round layer, put together as in diagram, covered with tube 16 stars. Head, neck and bill are styrofoam, wings and feet paper, legs triple straws taped together. Add a construction paper banner and a flower-trimmed hat!

2nd PRIZE: A SIT-DOWN SOLDIER

Second prize of a $15 gift certificate and CELEBRATE! II congratulations go to **Nora Thomas** of Las Vegas, Nevada for her clever toy soldier. We predict her ingenious use of the 3-D Rag Doll pan will be copied for sitting dolls of all kinds.

Nora chilled her cake, then carefully trimmed off the legs and feet and repositioned them in front of the doll. She trimmed off sides of hair and back bow and used those cake pieces to form hat. She iced the face smoothly and added tube 12 features, outlined uniform details with tube 2 and filled in with tube 16 stars.

3rd PRIZE: A "TIN" SOLDIER

Third prize and a gift certificate for $10 is won by **Mrs. Donald Camsky** of Bellaire, Ohio for her simple but adorable soldier cake. A toddler's delight!

Making him is so easy, it's actually fun. Stack up five 6" round layers, putting an 8" round of cardboard, iced blue, under the top layer for hat brim. Ice all layers white.

Pipe tube 48 stripes on sides of hat and three bottom layers, adding tube 18 stars at stripe ends and leaving one layer white for face. Use tube 18 again to pipe 4" long arms right on cake and add yellow military stripes to them with tube 46. Pipe white gloves with tube 8 and brush smooth.

For face, pipe tube 8 nose and add criss-cross eyes and smiley mouth with tube. 4. Use tube 4 again for buttons. Finish with 2-A button on top of hat.

HONORABLE MENTIONS

Three more cakes, too cute not to tell about, earned Honorable Mentions and a $5.00 Gift Certificate.

Marilyn McLain of St. Marys, Ohio, made a charming Lion's Head from a 12" round cake iced golden brown. Color Flow ears, nose and mouth were pressed on the center of the cake. Then Marilyn piped a tube 22 "mane" on the lion, starting near the top edge of the cake and working in toward the features. A final touch—whiskers of black shoestring licorice.

TWO irresistable blue whales swam into our contest, each made with the Egg-shaped Pan.

Catherine Jahnke of Middleport, New York, iced the cake smoothly with pale blue icing, piped a tail with tube 12, and added a white "wave" border all around the whale and white "water" spouting from his blow hole.

Gail Laing of Lancaster, California, trimmed a little off the bottom of the egg cake to tilt the whale up slightly, then inserted cardboard tail and fins. The entire cake was covered with tube 17 stars.

HOME FOR THE HOLIDAYS

Nothing quite equals the joy of coming home for the holidays, back to the kind of warm and loving welcome this old-fashioned kitchen stove symbolizes.

Make all Color Flow pieces at least 24 hours in advance to allow drying time. Tape wax paper over patterns and tape to cardboard, flowing major details of the design as separate pieces. Use tube 1 to outline the stove itself, the separate stove top, back grillwork, teakettle and turkey. With tube 2, outline separate side panels and sections of stove feet. Flow in with softened Color Flow icing. When dry, dot separate pieces with Color Flow icing and set in place on body of stove. Then overpipe scrollwork, lines on sides of stove, handles, teakettle and other details with tube 1, 2 or 4 as required.

Bake and ice a 8"x4" square cake. Pipe tube 7 brown scrollwork and balls freehand to frame corners of cake. Pipe tube 9 ball border around bottom of cake. Set Color Flow stove on dots of icing or flat sugar cubes on cake top. Serves 12.

PRETTY PETITS FOURS

Here's a shortcut to pretty petit fours for your next party. Bake 6"x2" petal cakes, chill thoroughly, and cut into eighths with a thin, serrated-edge knife. Cover each piece completely with Mock Fondant. To ice easily, set cake pieces on a wire rack and pour fondant over them, touching up bare spots with a spatula. Place cookie sheet underneath to catch run-off for re-use. Decorate quickly with tube 7 hearts and tube 2 dots. Each little cake makes eight petits fours.

MOCK FONDANT

   2 lbs. Wilton Dry Fondant
   2/3 cup water

Combine and stir thoroughly in saucepan. Let set 15 minutes, until fondant grains have dissolved and mixture is smooth. Place over low heat, stirring constantly, until mix thins. Test for proper consistency by dropping a spoonful of mixture back into pan. If it disappears by the count of 3, mixture is just right for coating cake. Tint with paste food color.

Scotland

THE FIRST SCOTTISH IMMIGRANTS arrived in the New World in 1707. Scottish merchants settled in colonial seaports, artisans and laborers went to the Southern tobacco-growing colonies or to New York. By 1860 over 100,000 Scots had settled in the United States.

American life and culture has borrowed much from Scotland. The Scots brought with them their close-knit family life and habit of thriftiness. We are all familiar with the writings of Robert Burns, Robert Louis Stevenson, Sir James Barrie and Sir Walter Scott.

Not the least of Scottish inventions is the game of golf which originated in Scotland in the 1400's.

This distinctive cake is ornamented by Scotland's Thistle. Directions for decorating start on page 154.

THE SPANISH PEOPLE have the distinction of being the founders of our oldest city, St. Augustine, Florida, in 1565.

It was on the west coast that Spanish people had the strongest influence. Spanish Franciscan missionaries were zealous in their efforts to teach and convert the Indians. By 1823, the Franciscans had built a chain of 21 missions along the coast. Many of these picturesque old buildings exist today.

Beginning in 1945, a large-scale migration of Spanish-speaking people from Puerto Rico came to the United States to seek a new and better life. These are our recent "Makers of America."

In honor of all citizens of Spanish descent, we have decorated this lacy Mantilla Cake. Directions start on page 154.

MAKERS
of
AMERICA

DENMARK  ITALY

Danish vikings explored the seas much more widely than did the other inhabitants of Western Europe and may have seen the New World as long as 500 years before Columbus made his discovery.

The Danish flag, a white cross on a red field, is the oldest national flag in continuous use in the world and dates back to the late 12th or early 13th centuries.

As "Makers of America", the Danes did not emigrate to these shores in appreciable numbers until the mid 1800's. Denmark abolished serfdom in 1788, an act which brought prosperity to the people. The Danish standard of living is one of the highest in the world, and few Danes are either very rich or very poor.

An especially interesting fact about Denmark is its celebration of U. S. Independence Day, appropriately observed each July 4th in a national park in Rebild. In 1911, a group of Danish-born Americans purchased Rebild Hills and gave it to the Danish government on the condition that American Independence Day be observed each year. This has been done.

Though the successful voyages of the Italian-born Columbus did not cause his fellow countrymen to set out for the New World in vast numbers during the early colonization of America. Italian craftsmen did settle in the colony of Virginia in 1610, to establish glass-making facilities.

The first Italian opera company performed in New York in 1832, brought to America by Lorenzo de Ponte. In addition to music, the Italians have brought with them a very rich heritage. For more than 2,000 years the homeland of Michelangelo, DaVinci and Verdi has developed an extremely rich culture. Italy's University of Bologna, established before 1100, indicates how far back this culture reaches.

While comparatively few Italians settled in America in the 18th and early 19th centuries, over 5,000,000 of Italy's citizens have since emigrated to America. Most settled in the major cities of the East and the valleys of the West. This cake which depicts Columbus's initial voyage to the New World honors Italian-Americans.

MAKERS
of
AMERICA

Instructions for decorating start on page 154.

DECORATING IN THE

MEXICAN
MANNER

DECORATING IN MEXICO is a complex art indeed. Mexican decorating has aspects of architecture, sculpture, theatre and even dressmaking. Our expert, Marithé de Alvarado, possesses talent in all these areas, and her cakes are high examples of the Mexican style.

The strongest impression one receives from Mexican cakes is of their theatrical quality. Elegantly clothed figures are grouped in settings of architecture or in formal gardens. Flowers are arranged formally. The cake is a stage for these tableaux, and is simply trimmed with beading or line work.

Mrs. Alvarado explains the Mexican art of sugar is built on three "pillars": pastillage, gum paste and royal icing.

Pastillage is used wherever strength is needed—for pillars, buildings and even as a base for dolls.

Gum paste is used to model dolls, rolled thin for their clothing, and for most flowers. Petals for flowers* are cut with special cutters, then the flower is assembled. A gum arabic solution is the glue that secures the gum paste parts.

Royal, or "hard", icing is used for some flowers, or parts of flowers, for trimming cakes and to join parts made of pastillage.

Mexican decorators use a heavy butter cake, similar to pound cake, covered with rolled fondant.

PASTILLAGE FORMULA
   1 tablespoon unflavored powdered
      gelatin
   4 ounces cold water
   5 ounces, plus 1 tablespoon
      granulated sugar
   2 pounds powdered sugar

*We regret that space does not permit detailed flower instructions by Mrs. Alvarado. You may substitute gum paste flowers from The Wilton Way of making Gum Paste Flowers.

Soften the gelatin in the cold water. Place the granulated sugar in a small sauce pan with water just to cover. Mix, then heat to boiling. Boil about 5 minutes without stirring until it forms a soft thread. Remove from heat and stir in softened gelatin. Stir until gelatin is completely dissolved. Add powdered sugar by spoonfuls, stirring constantly until like thick cream.

Heap remaining powdered sugar on formica table, make a well in the center and pour in the gelatin mixture. Mix with your hands until a *very soft* dough is formed. Now store in tightly-covered container.

When ready to use, knead more powdered sugar into dough, until you can roll it without its sticking to the table. Knead only portion you are going to use—keep rest well covered.

Roll the pastillage on a marble or formica surface with a heavy rolling pin, using cornstarch to prevent sticking. Be sure the pastillage is of even thickness. Cut the pieces, using a pattern, with a small, sharp knife. The pieces will usually dry in one day, but if humidity is high, dry them on one side for a day, then turn over and dry on the other side for a day.

Pastillage crusts quickly, so have patterns and knife ready before rolling.

Join pastillage pieces with medium consistency royal icing. Pipe a line of icing on one edge of one piece and immediately join second piece to it at correct angle. Then proceed with rest of pieces.

Any icing or painted trims on pastillage pieces should be done before joining.

ROYAL ICING FORMULA
    1 egg white
    ½ pound sifted powdered sugar
        strained, fresh lemon juice
Beat egg white by hand, using whisk, till thick and creamy. Continue beating while you add sugar. Thin with as much lemon juice as necessary for piping consistency.

GUM PASTE FORMULA
    2 cups sifted powdered sugar
    1 tablespoon gum tragacanth
    1½ tablespoons heavy glucose
    2 tablespoons (about) cold water
Mix sugar and tragacanth. Dip measuring spoon in water, spoon out glucose and add to dry ingredients. Immediately add water. Mix with hands until pliable. If too sticky, add powdered sugar; if too dry, add a few drops more water. This will depend on humidity. Place in tightly covered container and let season two or three days.

CAMPANARIO (bell tower)
"Simple in design, but with a real significance for a wedding—it's easy to make", says Mrs. Alvarado.

To reproduce this piece, 100 royal icing orange blossom buds are needed. Also needed are 50 gum paste orange blossoms made with Mrs. Alvarado's cutters, five 3" gum paste doves and three yards of white satin ribbon.

Make all the pastillage pieces for the tower, and dry them. Draw fine pencil lines on the square "brick" base, ⅓" apart. Paint each of the pillar pieces with a ⅓" gold stripe. Pipe icing cord with tube 3 on the arches and paint gold.

Model the bell from gum paste, using Mrs. Alvarado's bell mold. Dry and paint gold. The clapper is a hollow ball painted gold and wired to the bell.

Assemble the pieces in this order, using royal icing as "glue". 1. The square "brick" base. 2. The pillars. First stack the two squares that form the base, join the four sides of the pillars and set in position on base, add the two squares that form the capitals of the pillars. 3. Set the arches, upside down, on square roof and glue together. 4. Join sections of the large pyramid and four small pyramids. Dry and paint gold. 5. The square base for the large pyramid.

Final Assembly. Set arches on brick base and make light pencil mark to indicate position of pillars. Remove arches and glue pillars in base. Dry about one hour. Glue arches to pillars. Dry. Attach bell through hole in roof. Glue pyramid base to roof. Glue pyramids in position. Slide a thin 8" long bamboo stick through holes in arches to hold doves. Divide flowers and buds in two equal groups and make garlands by binding wire stems together with florist tape. Attach garlands to pillars with royal icing, holding in position with wire until dry.

ENSONACION (Dreaming)
This is a project for a decorator well practiced in modelling gum paste and a typical example of Mrs. Alvarado's work.

The oval cake is 9½" x 15", trimmed with cornelli and beading. It is placed on a 12" x 17½" wood rectangle covered with crushed foil. A pastillage oval, 4½" x 7½", serves as a base for the figure.

The pillar on which cupid is seated is 3" high, made from an Alvarado mold in pastillage. While still wet, it is centered with a slender 7" stick which projects 4" from the top of the pillar and serves as an armature for the figure. Hollow cornucopia is made in a mold from gum paste.

The cupid figure is made of gum paste and modelled almost entirely by hand. First the legs are shaped, each about 4½" long, and one by one placed on the pillar, then the body, 2½" long x 1½", and placed over the stick. When body is completely dry, shape the head in a mold and smooth onto the body. Pipe the hair with royal icing and tube 00, then attach the cornucopia, securing it with icing to front of chest. Finally, model the arms, attaching them to the shoulders with icing and holding with your hands until firmly set. Drape a 1" x 12" ribbon of gum paste around figure. Attach the cupid to the pastillage oval. When dry, fill the cornucopia with a gum paste flower arrangement.

Cupid Off His Pedestal—a gay cake inspired by Ensonacion. *See page 156.*

THE ART OF PULLED SUGAR

BY NORMAN WILTON

TRULY FASCINATING, pulled sugar is an art that produces spectacular decorating effects including satiny ribbons, bows and flowers. Pulled sugar requires practice, but the rewards are breathtaking.

Here's the equipment you will need:

a 40 to 60 gauge brass wire screen
an electric heater (guard removed)
a marble slab about 2 ft. x 3 ft.
a metal scraper
candy thermometer
a canvas strip about 3 ft. x 14"
a scissors
a small leaf mold

Before making pulled sugar, the cake should be iced in a thin coat of buttercream, then covered with poured fondant and assembled. Our spectacular wedding cake consists of 14", 10" and 6" round tiers, assembled with 8" separator plates and 5" iridescent Grecian Pillars. To decorate a cake of this size you need two recipes for a yield of 10 pounds. As a beginner, we suggest you make, and work with, just one recipe at a time. With the first recipe, do steps 1 through 11. Then complete remaining steps with second recipe. Before you attempt a tiered cake, plan to trim a smaller one. 10" x 12" cakes make ideal practice sizes. To decorate these smaller cakes you need only one recipe.

NOTE: pulled sugar will droop and lose its gloss in hot, humid weather, so *do this decorating only in dry, clear weather.*

PULLED SUGAR RECIPE

10 cups granulated sugar
2½ cups water
1 teaspoon cream of tartar

Add water to sugar and mix by hand until mixture is smooth and all lumps have dissolved. Add cream of tartar and cook to 312 deg. F, washing down the sides of the pan often with a wet pastry brush to keep crystals from forming. Note: the faster it's cooked, the whiter the mixture; the slower, the darker. If you plan to tint the sugar—the whiter the batch, the truer the color. Yield: 5 pounds

1. After sugar has cooked to correct temperature (usually 30 to 45 minutes), pour it onto a marble slab greased with lard.

2. Let cool a few minutes; then with a scraper, begin flipping sugar around edges, turning it over on all sides to keep it from sticking and to allow it to cool evenly. As you work quickly, you'll see the batch start to cool and the sugar begin to hold together.

3. Keep flipping the edges of the sugar and work it into a concentrated mass.

4. Let stand to cool to a pulling temperature, similar to that of pulling taffy.

5. When you can safely touch the sugar with your hands, pull and stretch it to make it pliable. As you start to pull, the sugar will loose its opaque quality and become more transparent.

After you've worked the sugar by hand, place it on the mesh screen in front of the electric heater to keep it at an even pulling temperature. A good idea, especially with a large batch of sugar, is to divide the batch before placing it in front of heater. Then when one batch seems somewhat stiffer, place it closer to the heater and work with the other batch. Always fold ends of standing sugar inward to keep heat concentrated throughout.

When decorating a cake with pulled sugar, the ribbons, garland drapes, ruffles and bows are made first, while the sugar is most pliable. The flowers are made last.

6. To make the tier-covering ribbons, cut off a piece of sugar about 7"x2" and place it on the canvas strip.

7. Begin pulling and stretching sugar from the ends, lengthening it as you work.

8. As you pull and stretch the sugar, it will acquire sheen and gloss. Now fold ribbon over, side by side, doubling its width.

9. Re-pull and stretch again, working fast before sugar loses its pliable quality.

10. When you have the length necessary to wrap a tier, cut off the uneven ends and wrap tier from front to back, overlapping at seam. Where the ribbon ends meet will be the back of the cake. Now follow the same procedure to wrap all three tiers with ribbon, covering each tier twice.

11. To make the base ruffles for the bottom and middle tiers, cut off a piece of sugar just as you did for the ribbons. Pull and stretch it on the canvas and, when it's about the length you desire, cut off the uneven ends, turn piece over, (shinier candy is underneath) and pinch ribbon together, hand over hand from one end to the other.

12. When strip is completely ruffled, wrap around tier base from front to back. If one piece of ruffle is not enough to wrap entire tier, make more sections and piece.

13. Cut off a 7" long, thin piece of sugar, pull and stretch it on the canvas; then cut it into 6" pieces and attach as garland drapes to top tier.

14. Cut off a long thin piece of sugar. This time instead of pulling, roll it back and forth on the canvas to form a rope twist.

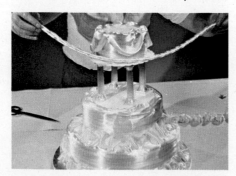

15. While sugar is still soft and pliable, wrap rope around base of top tier.

16. Now make lots of loop bows. Cut off a long thin piece of sugar, pull and stretch it on the canvas; then cut into 6" long pieces and fold over thumb, pressing ends together to form loop bows.

To decorate cake with bows, make separator ornament trims first. Remove the top tier and place a circular piece of unpulled sugar atop separator plate. Touch ends of loop bows to heater, then attach to sugar base working from center out. When arrangement is complete replace top tier.

For the ornament, press a piece of unpulled sugar around the base of a pair of White Birds and once again heat ends of loop bows to position around ornament.

17. To attach bows to cake, make three flat circles of unpulled sugar, each about 3" in diameter and heat to attach to tier sides. Next, heat ends of loop bows and attach to circles, working from outer edge in until circles are completely covered.

18. Cut a long thin piece of sugar and roll it on the canvas to form a rope. Wind the rope around a long stick or broom handle, and let stand a few minutes until sugar is cool enough to hold curves.

19. Pull off stick and place around top of middle tier. Heat a few small pieces of sugar to secure the curving vine to the separator plate at several points.

20. To make flowers, pinch off a small piece of sugar. Holding it in your left hand, press with your right thumb to form a cupped petal. Make five petals, pressing bases together to form a flower. Next, pull off a small piece of sugar and roll around base of artificial stamen to insert in flower center. To make leaves, cut off a piece of sugar and press into small leaf mold to shape. Touch bases to heater to position on cake for the finishing touches!

A cake in the grand tradition for a Christmas bride. Decorating directions, page 70.

THE DAY BEFORE
Christmas

HERE IS A CHRISTMAS STORY, never told before, of what happens on that longest day of the year, the day before Christmas.

All American children know the story of The Night Before Christmas, as told by Clement C. Moore. Our story starts just a little earlier, and its setting is much different. We are in Santa Claus' little cottage, on the North Pole.

The day before Christmas, Santa always has breakfast with his elves. It is a quick, early breakfast, oatmeal and milk, and as soon as everyone has finished eating, Santa makes a final inspection of the toys he'll bring to children all over the world that very night. Klick, the elf who is Santa's first helper, walks with him through the rows and rows of toys, packed and ready for the night-time trip. He has all the children's letters in his hand, to make sure that every child's dream is fulfilled. Then Mrs. Santa serves a picnic lunch to the elves in the work room, and Santa takes a cup of tea and goes to his bed for a nice long nap.

Now it's Klick's job to put up the Claus' Christmas tree, to hang the shiny Christmas balls, and drape the popcorn garlands the elves have strung through long December evenings.

Mrs. Claus has been busy in the kitchen, preparing the Christmas dinner for the next day. She stuffs a fat goose (Santa's favorite feast), gets a big ham ready for roasting, and fries three nice plump chickens. Cranberry sauce and mashed potatoes, pickled apples and pumpkin pie, and of course, the glorious plum pudding. The smells from the kitchen are deliriously delicious! She bakes a chocolate cake, and mixes a big bowl of oats and toasted corn for the reindeer.

Santa wakes up with a yawn and a roar. In shirt sleeves and vest, he rushes into the parlor to see the tree. "Best ever! Marvelous! Come, Sara!" Mrs. Claus comes in from the kitchen and can only throw up her hands in admiration. Klick smiles at their praise. He's made a little teddy bear for the youngest elf.

CONTINUE this story on the next page.

THE DAY BEFORE CHRISTMAS

Re-create the happy scene at your house on a luscious chocolate cake.

Make marzipan figures of Santa, Mrs. Santa and Klick, following directions on page 96. Then make the Christmas tree, using cone shape on ice cream cone as a base. Cover with tube 65 leaves, starting at bottom and working upward. When dry, dot with tube 4 balls and drape with tube 13 zigzag swags. Attach Color Flow star at top.

Mark a 7" circle on cardboard, tape wax paper over it and pipe the rug with tube 5, working from outside in, and keeping icing lines touching. Peel off paper after drying.

Bake a 10" x 4" two-layer cake and ice a glossy chocolate. Edge with tube 21 shell borders. Attach small candy canes on side of cake with icing and add red satin bows. Add round hard candies, trimmed with tube 16 drop flowers.

Set the rug in the center of the cake and place Christmas tree and figures. Call the children to come and see! Serves 14.

THE NIGHT BEFORE Christmas

READY FOR THE FLIGHT! The elves are harnessing the reindeer to the sleigh out near the stable. Santa's put on his red coat and mittens, boots and jaunty cap. Klick sits up on the balcony, ready to help Santa into his sleigh. Mrs. Claus runs out. "Goodbye, goodbye! Be careful! Hurry home!"

An hour after Santa leaves, the little cottage is quiet. The elves are sleeping soundly in their cots in the big attic room. Their dreams are like those of children everywhere on Christmas Eve.

Mrs. Santa slumbers on the sofa in the parlor, ready to wake the instant the reindeer touch ground at daybreak in the front yard. Then there'll be the jingle of bells, the shouted greetings and bear hugs, the passing round of mugs of hot cocoa as the elves tumble pell-mell down the narrow attic stairs—

THE NEXT CHAPTER needs no words. It's every child's vision of the magic of Christmas Morning. The presents, the magnificent Christmas tree, the garlands, the glory. Merry Christmas!

GERMANY, as we all know, is nowhere near the North Pole! But what more appealing and imaginative dwelling could the Claus family choose than the truly storybook German Gingerbread house? The Germans have enriched both the celebration and spirit of Christmas with the highly ornamented tree (*O Tannenbaum*) and the lovely *"Silent Night"*. Elves from the Black Forest have also been credited with making many of the toys Santa carries down chimneys all over the world.
Directions for Santa's cottage, page 154.

Christmas morning

Decorating directions are on page 95

HERE IS YOUR CHANCE to try some of the cherished candy recipes of Master Chef Larry Olkiewicz, pastry chef at Chicago's Drake Hotel. These superb liqueur-and-creme filled chocolates are a specialty of Swiss confectioners and impossible to buy in this country. Yet you'll find them easy to create, with Chef Olkiewicz's clear directions and plastic candy molds. Make some as a sweet surprise for your family or friends this Christmas! All of these recipes yield 120 to 150 pieces.

A basic ingredient in these candies is tempered chocolate. To prepare, heat water in bottom of 1½ quart double boiler. For each recipe, use 3 pounds chocolate, cut or broken into small chunks and left to soften at room temperature. When water is 175°F. remove from heat and place chocolate (one cup at a time) in top of double boiler to melt. Stir every few minutes until melted at temperature of 110°F. Remove from heat and cool until almost stiff. Then reheat chocolate for molding. Reheat dark chocolate to 90-92°F., light milk chocolate to 86-88°F. Amount of chocolate in pan for dipping should be twice the height of the piece being dipped. Left-over chocolate can be used again.

Fondant is another ingredient in some of these recipes. This recipe yields 3½ pounds, but it will keep at room temperature for weeks.

WILTON FONDANT
    3½ pounds granulated sugar
    2 cups water
    ½ pound glucose
Combine in a large, heavy saucepan and heat until sugar is dissolved. When syrup looks clear, wash down side of pan with brush dipped in warm water. Repeat several times. Increase heat and boil until it reaches 240°F. on a candy thermometer. Pour mixture onto a marble slab and let cool until lukewarm. When mixture begins to set and you can comfortably touch it at the edge, start to "work it" with a candy scraper. With your hand in palm up position, and blade of scraper lying almost flat, push under edge of mass and move toward center. Lift as much as possible each time and fold over onto rest with circular motion. Repeat over and over. Soon mass will begin to thicken and whiten. Continue pushing, lifting and folding. When it becomes so stiff and thick you can stand the scraper straight up in it (usually about 4 minutes) pile in a mound cover with a damp cloth, let stand a few minutes. Then knead like bread dough and very quickly it will soften and become smooth and creamy. This can be used immediately. (Keep covered with damp cloth whenever it is not being used, to prevent its drying out.) Store at room temperature in air-tight container. To use, warm the portion you need in double boiler (do not let water boil), stirring constantly, until pourable—98°F.

APRICOT BRANDY SQUARES
Use square plastic molds to make hollow candy bodies. Fill molds with tempered chocolate up to rim, turn over immediately onto screen set over wax paper. Let excess chocolate run off, set upright and scrape off excess chocolate. Place molds in refrigerator and let cool about 10 minutes until squares slip out easily. Place on tray, hollow side up. Add filling, leaving room at the top for chocolate covering.

Filling
    8 ounces fondant
    ¾ to 1 ounce apricot brandy
    15 dried apricot halves, chopped in
        small pieces and soaked overnight
        in apricot brandy
Dilute fondant with brandy and mix in fruit. Add more brandy if needed to reach proper consistency. Put fondant into paper cone with cut tip and fill hollow molds, then let fondant set about 10 minutes until crust forms. Then cover with thin layer of chocolate from cone with cut tip.

CHERRY HEERING ROUNDS
Prepare molds using same chocolate molding process as above.

Filling
    8 ounces fondant
    1 ounce Cherry Heering
Dilute cold fondant with Cherry Heering to a runny consistency, adding more liqueur if needed. Fill molds, leaving enough room at top for thin chocolate covering. Let filling dry about 10 minutes, then cover with soft chocolate from cone with cut tip.

ZURICH GRAND MARNIER CUPS
Prepare fluted cups of chocolate in same manner as Apricot Brandy Squares and fill with Grand Marnier Creme.

Grand Marnier Creme
    5 ounces butter
    5 ounces Grand Marnier
    20 ounces tempered milk chocolate
Whip butter and Grand Marnier together with wire whisk or hand beater, gradually add chocolate and whip at slow speed until well blended but not too fluffy. Put in paper cone with cut tip and fill cups to top. Level with small spatula. Dust with cocoa powder sifted through fine seive.

COGNAC TRUFFLES
    8 ounces almond paste
    2 ounces confectioners sugar
Mix together and roll out; cut out rounds about ½" in diameter and ⅛" thick. Let stand till dry.

Creme Filling
    6½ ounces butter
    3½ ounces Curacao
    1½ ounces Cognac
    18 ounces tempered milk chocolate
With wire whisk or hand mixer, whip all ingredients together at low speed until thick and fluffy. Drop filling from tube 9 onto prepared rounds, to make small mounds. Refrigerate about 20 minutes, then dip in chocolate. Decorate with chocolate spiral.

RIGISPITZEN
These dainty chocolate mountains are inspired by towering Mt. Rigi, high above Lucerne. Use the same mix of almond paste and confectioners sugar as for Truffles. Roll out, cut ½" rounds, dry.

Continued on page 156

Christmas Candy

HOW THE EXPERTS DO IT
LARRY OLKIEWICZ

KEEP THE CHRISTMAS CUSTOMS

One of the cosiest customs of Christmas is hanging the stockings the night before. Here's a new way to honor the custom with a whole family of stockings in cake.

In advance, make gold medal and ribbon for garter using pattern and Color Flow method. Outline with tube 1 and flow in thinned Color Flow icing. Make tube 225 drop flowers.

Now bake two 9" x 13" x 2" cakes. Chill or freeze to make cutting easier. Then cut out stockings, fitting patterns on top of cakes to use all available space.

Following patterns, outline designs on stockings with tube 2 stringwork. Fill in all designs, tops and sides, with tube 16 stars in appropriate colors. Give the snowman tube 2 eyes, mouth and nose. On baby's striped sock, use two rows of stars for each stripe. Pipe tube 104 ruffles on socks for girls in the family. Accent pink and green striped one with tube 225 drop flowers. Attach the gold medal and ribbon to plaid stocking with dots of icing. Arrange on tray for all to admire.

IN THE LATE 1800's and early 1900's more than one million Swedes settled in the United States, setting up new homes all the way from Delaware to Minnesota, and as far west as Washington. Many of their countrymen emigrated as early as 1830, somewhat remarkable considering Sweden has long been a democratic country with the oldest (1809) written constitution in force in Europe.

In Sweden, the Christmas season opens with the Festival of Lights on December 13, St. Lucia (or Lucy) Day. The role of St. Lucy is played by a young girl of the household to herald the return of "more daylight hours" to the dark Swedish winter. The designated St. Lucia rises early on the festive day, dons the traditional white dress and a crown of greens that carries lighted candles. St. Lucia then serves the members of her family coffee and St. Lucia buns. A charming custom! Directions for St. Lucia cake on page 155.

SWEDEN

In a reenactment of the age-old harvest festival, the American Indian joins the early settler in giving thanks for good crops. The first officially decreed Thanksgiving Day was celebrated July 30, 1623, by the Plymouth colonists. Universal acceptance came in 1863, when President Lincoln proclaimed the last Thursday in November as "a day of thanksgiving and praise to our beneficient Father".

Americana: THE FIRST THANKSGIVING

Here is Tom Turkey in full splendor! It is undoubtedly the American Indian to whom we are indebted for our introduction to this magnificent bird. The Indians, as marks of friendship, brought wild turkeys to the earliest American settlers for major celebrations. Now the proud gobbler has become synonymous with the festive and fragrant Thanksgiving feast. Instructions for both Thanksgiving cakes on page 156.

Americana: THE THANKSGIVING TURKEY

HAPPY CAKES for the HOLIDAYS

Quick to fashion because the ingenious trims are made in advance!

Glowing color makes them pretty as a picture.

A SMILING SANTA

What a jolly sight on Christmas night! Fast and easy if you remember to make the gum paste eyes and banner before the holiday rush. See page 32 for recipe.

Prepare banner first. Roll out gum paste and cut a strip, 7" long x 1¼" wide for tint. Lay banner across tree pan to dry so it will fit curve of cake. Cut ½" diameter circles for Santa's eyes at the same time. When banner is dry, write "Merry Christmas" with tube 1.

Bake a single cake mix in a flat Christmas Tree pan. Ice very thickly with buttercream, so the sculptered curves on top do not show. Mound icing slightly to define stomach, arms and mittens. Set on foil-covered base, cut slightly larger, and fill in face, hat, jacket, sleeves, pants and boots with tube 16 stars.

Position eyes on Santa's face, then pipe his cherry nose and round cheeks with tube 9 and flatten with a finger. Curve his merry smile with tube 5 and glaze eyes with corn syrup.

Pull out flowing hair, beard and twirly mustache with tube 16. Swirl fur trim on cap, cuffs, jacket and boots with tube 9. Top cap with a marshmallow tassel on a toothpick, and Santa's ready to serve 12 delighted true believers!

A FLOWERING STAR

Cake and conversation piece in one— our delicious star cake topped with Christmas trees shaped of icing poinsettias. Cleverest ever, but so very simple.

Begin by making the poinsettias. Use flower nail 9, leaf tube 352 and deep red icing. First pipe a circle of eight 1-inch petals, then top with 4 more petals, piped in between first ones. Next, add a row of five ¾-inch petals and one more of three ⅜-inch petals. Center with tube 1 green dot stamens, pipe yellow dots atop them and finally add tiny dots of red color with a pointed artist's brush. Set aside to dry.

Next outline and fill in flower pot patterns from CELEBRATE! II Pattern Book, using the Color Flow method.

With flowers and pots ready, prepare the cake. Bake a two-layer cake in a pair of Star Pans, using a single mix. Ice and edge with tube 17 star borders.

Now "plant" trees. Shape each tree of six poinsettias and position, using picture as your guide. Pipe trunks with tube 46. For side-of-cake trees, put pots on mounds of icing, so they will stay in place.

Your star cake is ready to shine at any holiday party—and serve 12 beautifully.

THE GLOW OF HANUKAH

The burning of candles in the 9-branch Menorah, celebrates an ancient victory of the Jews over a tyrant who tried to make them abandon their religious beliefs.

Thus, Hanukah is actually a celebration of religious freedom and a holiday with meaning for all people. To honor it, we've created a special Hanukah cake with a built-in Menorah.

To fashion it, begin by preparing Menorah design, covering pattern from CELEBRATE! II Pattern book with wax paper and tracing it with tube 17 royal icing rope. Dry thoroughly, then pipe royal icing points on back and dry again.

Ice a two-layer cake, 8" square and 4" high and trace 6-pointed Jewish star pattern from same pattern book on top. Pipe latticework within outline. Lattice will be three layers thick in center of star. Add bead border with tube 1.

Position Menorah on cake side, pushing in back points to secure. Add colorful Hanukah candles in Crystal Clear Holders just behind tops of Menorah arms.

Divide rest of cake sides into 4ths and pipe tube 14 double drapes from mark to mark. Use tube 16 to pipe star accents and top shell border. Circle base of cake with tube 17 rosettes.

You're ready to light the candles and serve 12 guests.

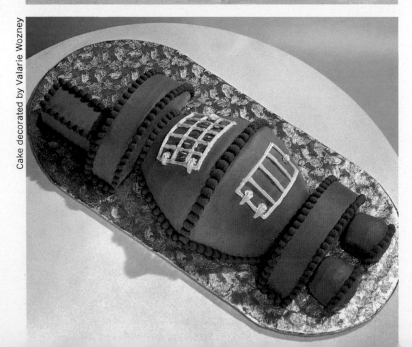

CONGRATULATIONS, YOU WON!

Our contest for Anytime Cakes—"any cake you think is a winner"—brought forth hundreds of the most unusual ideas of all. We thought these were the best! Our judges chose these winners.

FIRST PRIZE of a $25 gift certificate and CELEBRATE! II congratulations goes to **Marilyn Ranger** of Van Nuys, California. Cake decorating and oil painting are her favorite hobbies, so she combined the two arts in this winning cake. She created an 11" x 15" sheet cake version of a framed Renoir painting that captures the delicate coloring and dream-like mood of the original to perfection! Displayed on a real wood easel, it was given extra support by a thick cardboard base. Tinted icings were smoothed on with a flexible knife; frame was iced on, then piped with scrolls.

SECOND PRIZE of a $15 gift certificate is awarded to **Mabel Crown** of Rockville, Maryland for her lovely altar wedding cake with a most unusual construction. She placed 2 each of 8", 12" and 16" square cakes side-by-side and stacked. The top cake that forms the altar is a 6" square cake cut in half to make a 12" x 3" shape placed end-to-end. A styrofoam half circle holds lacy arches and a sugar mold cross and bible. On the bible she wrote the lovely Old Testament quotation that starts, "Whither thou goests, I will go . . ."

THIRD PRIZE of a $10 gift certificate is won by **Dorothy Weidner** of Alta Loma, Texas for her amusing Pot Bellied Stove cake. She split a Wonder Mold cake lengthwise and positioned the two halves for stove's basic shape. A one-inch strip cut off each end formed smokestack, and an 8" round cake cut in half became stove's top and base. A cupcake cut in half formed legs. She iced all with chocolate, added tube 4 "door" and "grate" and shell edging. Pink roses trimmed her cake board. A charming bit of "Americana".

HONORABLE MENTION

Prizes of $5 gift certificates go to each of three wonderful runners-up!

Sandy Sewell of Bartow, Florida submitted a glorious Flower Garden wedding cake. The 3-tiered cake had sides covered in white basket weaving and was decked with colorful gum paste flowers, glazed for an exquisite porcelain-like look.

Carroll M. Corcoran of Crystal, New Mexico made the happiest Housewarming Cake we've ever seen. House-shaped cake is given a happy smile with Color Flow window "eyes" and a door "nose and mouth". A gum paste "electric blanket" covers roof and "plugs in" to side of house.

Jada Thadani of Houston, Texas, decorated a clever Peacock Cake. She placed two sheet cakes together, cut out shape from her own pattern and covered it with a rainbow of colorful icing stars.

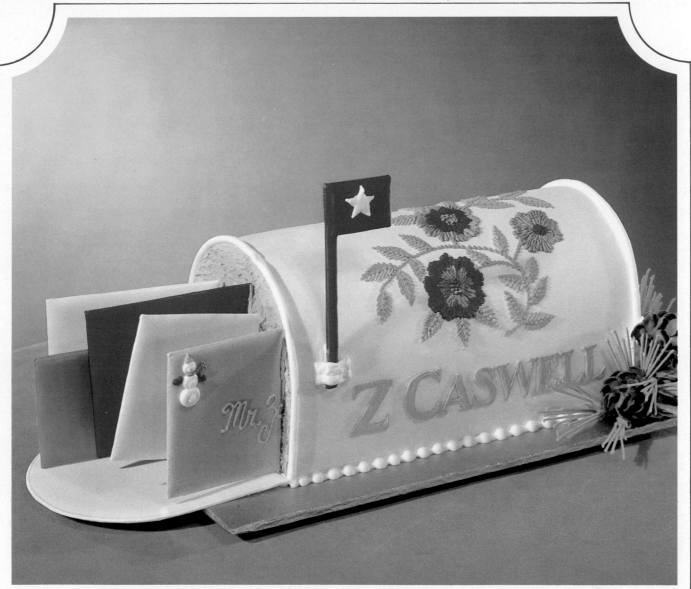

Americana: THE RURAL MAILBOX

The walk to the roadside mailbox was the pleasantest part of the day for many Americans a generation or two ago. The floral design on our mailbox is adapted from one of the many colorful patterns woven into the carpet Zeruah Guernsey embroidered for her hope chest in 1835. The Caswell Carpet is on display in New York's Metropolitan Museum of Art.

To decorate, cover CELEBRATE! II patterns for lid, flag, star and envelopes with wax paper, outline with tube 2 and fill in with Color Flow icing. Next pipe several tube 103 pinecones (directions start page 90), then use tube 1 to pipe pine needles on wax paper.

For the mailbox, bake a 4" x 4" x 8" loaf cake and trim the top for a rounded effect. Ice the open front blue, patting for a stuc-co effect, then ice the rest of the cake white. Edge both ends and do base border with tube 4. Now place the flower pattern on top of the cake and prick through the design. Pipe flowers with tube 1 using short strokes and a "satin stitch" technique. Pipe leaves in same manner and stem in "chain stitch" fashion. Then use tube 1 to outline letters and brush in thinned icing.

Attach star to flag with icing; then pipe a spike of icing on back of flag base and, when dry, push into cake and pipe two tube 6 icing strips on front to secure. With more icing, position Color Flow mailbox lid, envelopes, pine cones and needles, adding snowman and addressings to letters with tubes 1 and 2. Serves 8.

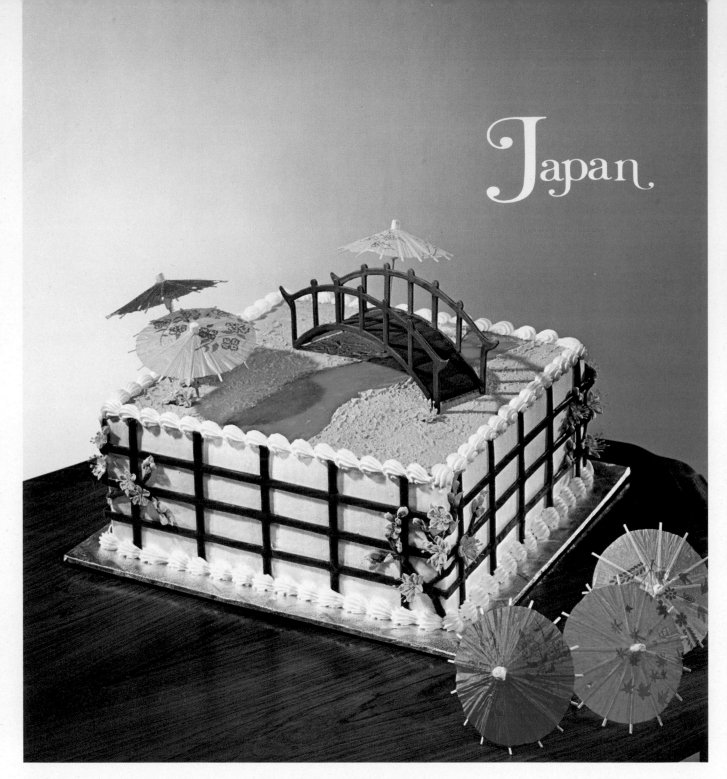

Japan

Unlike the citizens of many Western European countries, practically no Japanese appear among the "Makers of America" until late in the 19th century. The reason for this is easily explained: until 1885 the Japanese government allowed no immigration. After this date, many Japanese settled in the state of California and in Hawaii, a territory of the U.S. from 1898 until it attained statehood in 1959. They proved to be very good citizens, many serving with honor during World War II in the 100th Infantry Battalion and other distinguished units.

Directions for this Japanese tableau cake start on page 155.

Since 1820, over three and one-half million Russians have emigrated to the United States. They have brought with them a very rich culture from a country that has given the world the works of such great artists as Chekhov, Tolstoy, Dostoevsky and Tchaikovsky. Among the many Russian immigrants who clearly must be included among the "Makers of America" are Irving Berlin, Igor Stravinsky, Alexander de Seversky, Igor Sikorsky and Selman Wakesman. This poetic "Swan Lake" cake does honor to Russian-Americans who have made a great culture a part of the fabric of America. Directions start on page 156.

MAKERS
of
AMERICA

RUSSIA

POLAND

THE UNITED STATES has always had a strong link with Poland. During the American Revolution, two great Poles fought on the side of the American colonists for freedom. Thaddeus Kosciusko offered his services to the Continental Congress in 1776. He built the fortifications at Saratoga and along the Hudson at West Point. Casmir Pulaski joined Washington in 1777 and was made Brigadier General in charge of cavalry. He died of wounds suffered in the siege of Savannah.

Freedom-loving Poles have come to America by the hundreds of thousands. In 1830, Congress alloted 36 sections of Illinois farm land to Poles fleeing the Polish revolution. Others settled in Connecticut, New York and Pennsylvania and, farther west, in Michigan.

The melodies of Chopin, Paderewski and Rubinstein are familiar to all American ears. And everybody loves the polka!

Poland's great Copernicus was the founder of present-day astronomy. His bold theories helped the United States send men to the moon centuries later.

This cake was decorated to honor freedom-loving Polish-Americans. Directions start on page 156.

MAKERS
of
AMERICA

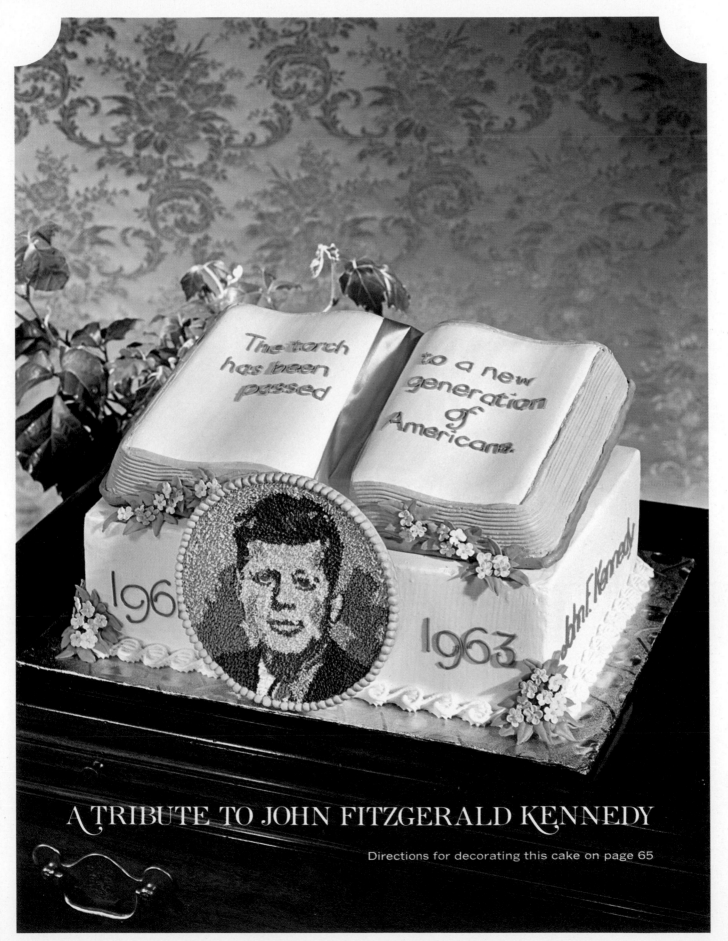

The torch has been passed to a new generation of Americans.

1963
1963
John F. Kennedy

A TRIBUTE TO JOHN FITZGERALD KENNEDY

Directions for decorating this cake on page 65

143

THE JOLLIEST CAKES FOR THE MERRIEST PARTIES

THE WEEK between Christmas and New Year's day can be just a little too long for out-of-school youngsters. Take everyone for a tramp in the snow, a spin on the ice, or an igloo-building adventure in the park. Come home to hot cocoa and one of these breathtaking holiday cakes.

A ROMP IN THE SNOW. Make the Eskimo children from marzipan and dry about 48 hours. (Recipe and directions, page 96.)

Build the igloo from a cake baked in a half-ball pan, set on a one-layer 6" round cake. The igloo entrance is made from a cake baked in an 8-ounce juice can with one side of cake flattened and end trimmed to fit against ball cake.

Bake a 12" two-layer round cake and ice smoothly—green on sides, white on top. Assemble igloo on top of cake and ice. Pipe tube 8 ball border at base of cake. Pipe "blocks" on igloo with tube 3. Now pile fluffy boiled icing on top of igloo and cake, pulling down for icicle effect.

Sprinkle generously with edible glitter. Pipe tube 3 clear icicles with piping gel. Place Eskimo boy and girl on top of cake. Serve to 28 wide-eyed children.

THE MOST POPULAR COUPLE in the world is Mr. and Mrs. Santa Claus! Here they are in a portrait made of cake and icing.

Make the holly leaves with a pattern and Color Flow method. Dry on Flower Formers. Bake cakes in a set of bell pans, using one mix. Ice in white buttercream. Prick patterns on cakes and outline color areas with tube 3. Now fill in Santa's coat and cap and Mrs. Santa's dress with tube 17 stars. Toothpick a marshmallow to top of Santa's cap and cover it with stars also. Pipe tube 12 eyes and button noses, and give each a tube 4 smile. Swirl Santa's eyebrows, mustache and beard with tube 19. Make Mrs. Santa's hair-do with tube 233 and give her a tube 1 ringlet. Finish her dress with a tube 103 bow and tube 12 buttons. Dress up the happy couple with holly leaves and pipe tube 6 red berries. Serves 12 friends.

Commonsense

FOR THE CAKE DECORATOR

NORMAN WILTON has perhaps had a greater influence on cake and food decorating than any other decorator in the United States, and possibly the world. While he firmly believes in being a perfectionist, he does not believe in stifling any decorator's creativity with a set of inflexible rules that might turn what should be an enjoyable art form into a drudge job.

Mr. Wilton feels it is essential to master basic decorating techniques, but readily agrees—once mastered—they can be modified. In short, Norman Wilton knows decorating should be—and can be—both pleasurable and perfectionist. *Commonsense For Cake Decorators* is intended to make it easier for decorators at all levels of skill to get the maximum artistry from their efforts, and to have fun doing it!

COLOR: THE DECORATOR'S MAGIC

WOULD YOU BELIEVE that the four cakes on the opposite page are identical in construction and border trim? The top and side trims do vary—but the real difference is COLOR.

Even our own staff did not realize at first that the four cakes were so similar. Each projects a distinct personality through the skillful use of color.

The cake for baby is dainty and sweetly simple. Soft yellow is set off by white borders and tiny white and yellow flowers with accents of green.

The lavender and green birthday cake gives a sophisticated, feminine effect. The colors of the two tiers are unified by the crisp white borders. The note of aqua in the flowers adds a third dimension to this fashionable cake.

Red and blue, forthright and strong, sing out on the patriotic cake. The two colors are used full strength on a white background to play against each other.

The holiday cake is iced in brilliant but soft hues of orange and deep pink, set off by the yellow-green of the holly leaves. The effect is festive, rich and glowing.

COLOR FOR THE DECORATOR

For most of us, most of the time, color is something to feel, to enjoy, to be moved by—just to see. The sparkling blue of a winter sky, the blending pastels of a bouquet, the brilliant rich hues of a hardwood forest in autumn—all are accepted with pleasure and delight.

To the decorator, color is perhaps the most important element in the effect of their creations. Even for those with a trained eye, it is necessary to observe, experiment and study color and the effects that one color may have upon another.

Objects for observation are all around us. Flowers, paintings, fabrics, attractive wearing apparel. Take time to observe combinations of colors. They will give you ideas for decorating. Your eye will be sharpened and your enjoyment in just seeing will be increased.

Experiment with dabs of colored icing placed next to each other on white cardboard. Try different combinations to see which appeals to you most. Make some icings bright and deep, others pastel. Put your efforts away for a few days, then look at them again to see if your opinion is the same. Save the combinations you like best for use in future decorating projects. You'll have fun with these experiments, and your cakes will be prettier and more expressive.

No matter how simple the cake—COLOR is the magic ingredient that gives it beauty and personality.

DECORATING THE CAKES

Each of the four cakes consists of one 6" x 3" round tier and one 10" x 4" round tier. All 10" tiers are decorated with tube 16 shells for base and top borders, and tube 19 scrolls with tube 16 star trims around sides. All 6" tiers are decorated with tube 16 shells at base, top and sides, and tube 19 scrolls at base between the vertical shell rows.

BABY CAKE. Pipe tube 224 and 225 drop flowers with tube 2 centers, and tube 65 leaves. Set aside to dry. Attach some flowers and leaves to florist wires with icing.

Position flowers on the 10" tier top with icing and trim with tube 65 leaves; then place a piece of styrofoam in Baby Bassinet and insert wired flowers and leaves. Set bassinet atop cake and write out baby's welcome wishes on the 10" tier side with tube 1.

MISS SOPHISTICATE. Pipe tube 103 wild roses with tube 1 stamens. Allow to dry.

Then attach flowers to 10" tier sides with icing, trimming with tube 65 leaves. Next, mound icing on the cake top, push in a tall taper and then attach flowers around candle to cover icing and trim with tube 65 leaves. Position Push-In Candle Holders around 10" tier sides.

BICENTENNIAL TRIBUTE. Mold stars with white, red and blue-tinted sugar. Put two stars together with florist wire between them, using icing as "glue." Sprinkle with Edible Glitter. Half-fill Uncle Sam Hat with icing, insert a circle of styrofoam, and push in wired stars.

Write out birthday wishes with tube 2 and position star bouquet atop cake.

HOLIDAY BRIGHT. To decorate the cake aglow with holiday color, use Celebrate! II pattern to outline leaves with tube 2 and fill in with softened Color Flow Icing. Dry leaves on Flower Formers.

Attach leaves to 10" tier sides with icing; then mound icing on the cake top, push in a tall candle and arrange more leaves around taper to cover icing.

Each of the four cakes yields 20 party-sized servings.

MANY of you have asked for the methods used by the CELEBRATE! staff in mixing colors. Norman Wilton discusses this subject on page 152.

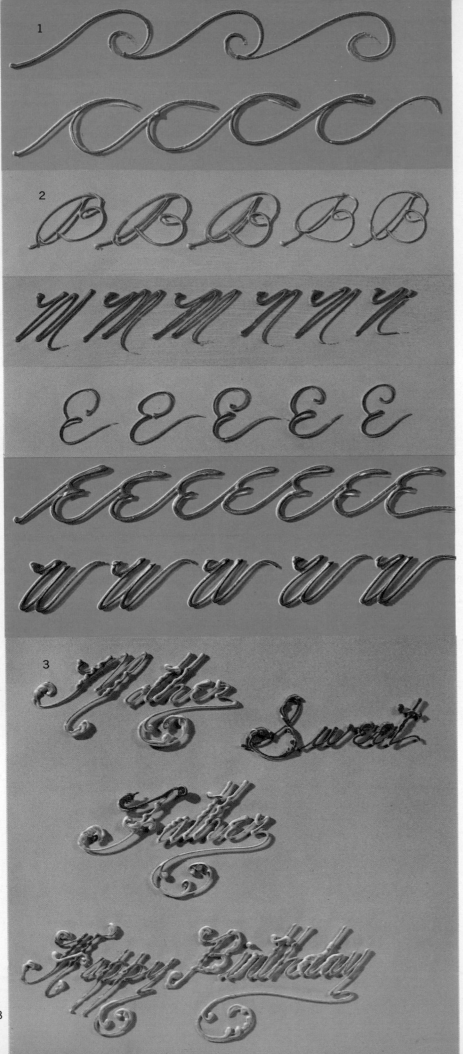

THE THREE SECRETS OF BEAUTIFUL SCRIPT

Anyone can write decorative wishes across a party cake, regardless of penmanship, because writing on a cake is entirely different from writing on paper. Whether your handwriting is large and lavish, or small and hard-to-read—you can learn to write beautifully in icing if you follow these three secrets to success:

1. USE YOUR ENTIRE ARM. Since you are not confined to a single line on a sheet of paper, you can use a relaxed movement of your entire arm, not just your fingers, to form individual letters. This technique adds roundness to each letter and more clarity to each word.

2. HAVE THE ICING AT THE CORRECT CONSISTENCY. For the best writing results, the icing must be thin enough to flow and stretch with your arm movements. Piping gel, which is often used for writing across a cake top, is an ideal choice since it is already at the proper consistency. Gives a pretty shine, too.

3. PRACTICE. Like any other cake decorating technique, writing requires practice before perfection can be achieved. Here are some exercises to try on the back of a cake pan or cookie sheet. Use writing tube 2 and follow the three secrets to beautiful script in each exercise. Check yourself to be certain you are moving your entire arm and are not practicing in a cramped position.

PRACTICE BASIC FORMS

1. Holding tube 2 almost horizontal to your practice surface, squeeze and move tube up, around and under—up, around and under—in a series of graceful curves. Try to keep a steady, even pressure and a smooth continuous motion. Next practice curves with a downward stroke. First squeeze out an upward stroke, then bring tube down, curve around, finish up and repeat, again keeping a continuous, even pressure.

PRACTICE CAPITAL LETTERS

2. In any ornamental script, capital letters are very important because their size gives character and versatility to the special message of the day. In practicing these letters, use a smooth, continuous movement of the arm for even strokes.

ORNAMENT THE LETTERS

3. After you've practiced the basic forms and letters, you're ready to add the flourishes that give your cake-written messages added flair. Here, the decorative touches are added on the downward strokes of the letters. For example, in forming the letter "M," make the upward motion first, then pipe the downward stroke making pressure stops as you squeeze. These hesitations add a distinctive look.

148

HOW TO IMPROVISE SIMPLE BORDERS

Any basic border takes on a new and decorative look when you use a different tube. Here the tubes in the Essex Series, with their deep cut designs, provide interesting design effects to otherwise simple borders.

1. Essex tube 347, held with the single opening side up, provides an overpiped look to a basic curve and double "i" motion border.

2. Here tube 347, again held with the single opening side up, gives a dramatically different overpiped effect to a reverse shell border.

3. Essex tube 320 gives a rich, embellished look to this simple border—a series of curves with circular loop motions between.

This is a border which can be used to advantage wherever a look of Old World elegance is wanted.

4. Essex tube 362 gives a rich, deep ribbed detail to a basic shell border. Then the use of tube 352 provides added interest. By holding Essex tube sideways, pipe between the shells a series of unique leaf shapes that add a strikingly new dimension.

5. Here Essex tube 353 provides a standout effect for a series of curves. Then for the finishing touch, tube 352 is used once again to add leaves between curve points. Again, the addition of the leaf shapes gives the completed border a fresh, new look.

DROP FLOWERS . . . QUICK WAY TO LAVISH BORDERS

Besides different tubes giving basic borders added interest, drop flowers can turn a plain decoration into something really special—and do it quickly and easily. Since you make drop flowers in advance; they're all ready to be positioned on garlands and borders for instant appeal. The borders below are trimmed with tube 224 flowers.

1. Here a series of circle outlines made with tube 13 are overpiped with reverse shells for a feathered effect; then drop flowers at base and top.

2. Overpiping a single tube 2 drop string border with a zigzag motion is a perfect garland base for adding drop flowers and tube 2 bows.

3. In this side border, tube 14 is used for a curving guideline. Overpiping the curves with tube 14 circles made in the opposite direction gives a special touch to the otherwise simple decoration, while drop flowers positioned in the curves with icing add the final fancy flair.

4. Here a basic tube 2 curving vine border is dotted with drop flowers and trimmed with tube 65s leaves, making a sweet cake surrounding easier than ever.

—NORMAN WILTON

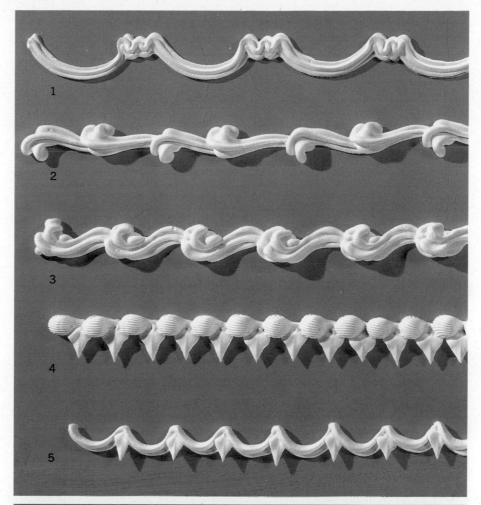

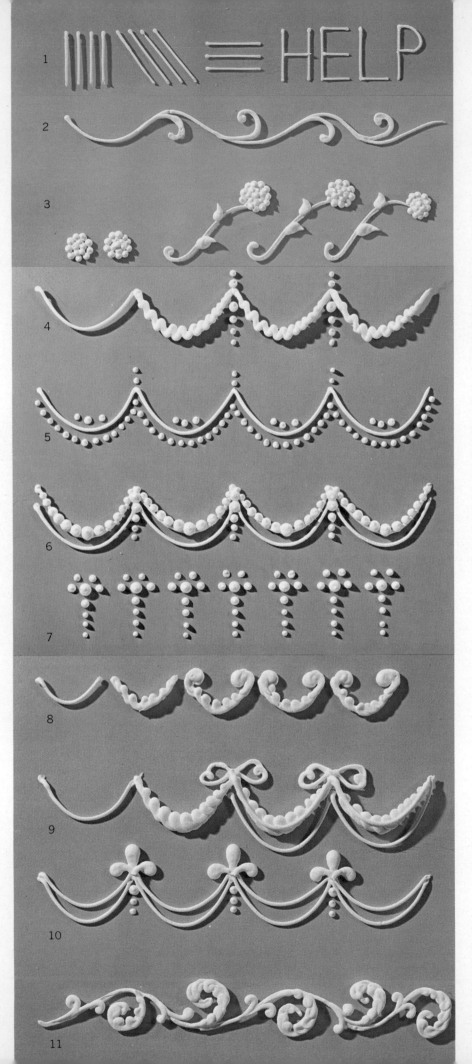

WRITING TUBES

Besides spelling out happy wishes across a party cake top, writing tubes are also ideal for decorating cakes with graceful curving borders, scrollwork, stringwork and lavish garlands. Here are examples of just a few of the decorative effects you can achieve with tubes 1 through 6.

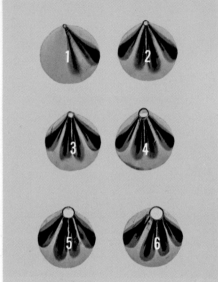

1. With writing tube 1 draw a series of short vertical, slanted and horizontal lines. Then print out letters which are simply combinations of these lines.

2. With tube 2, squeeze out a scroll ending with an undercurved stroke. Then place tube at top of curve and squeeze out another scroll ending with an upturned stroke. Repeat for a reverse scroll border.

3. Tube 2 dot flowers start with center dot. Then a ring of dots is added. For extra flourish, draw tube 2 stems, top with dot flowers and stroke stems with leaves.

4. With writing tube 3 squeeze out a single row of drop strings, overpipe with a zigzag motion and decorate with dots of icing for a quick side border.

5. Another tube 3 single drop string row has curves dotted below, above and at peaks for a different effect.

6. Now with tube 3 pipe a double row of drop strings, above top string, add icing dots—light to heavy to light pressure—then decorate spaces between curves with vertical dot rows.

7. For a fast, easy side trim squeeze out vertical dot rows with tube 3—heavy to

150

light pressure—then frame top with double dots on each side.

8. Here a row of tube 3 curves are overpiped with a circular motion and "c" swirls are added for a feathery side cake border.

9. A frilly side border for any tier cake starts with a tube 3 drop string row which is overpiped with a circular motion—light to heavy to light pressure—and ornamented with tube 3 stringwork on top and below. Dainty bows add the finishing touch.

10. A double row of tube 3 stringwork is embellished with fleur-de-lis and icing dots for a stunning side cake garland.

11. Here tube 3 reverse scrolls take on added flair when curves are overpiped with a circular motion and decorative little branch strokes are drawn in to compliment the reverse scrolls.

12. A graceful grapevine makes a festive, flowing side border.
First, pipe a tube 4 curving vine, stroking tiny branches into the curves where grapes will be added. Next overpipe branches with outlines for grape bunches. Apply heavy pressure to build up icing to fill in these outlines. Now squeeze out shell-motion grapes, starting from the edge and working into center of bunch. As a finishing touch pipe spiral tendrils between grape bunches and you have a fancy-fruit border.

13. Here tube 4 produces a bulb border ideal for top or base of cake. Just pipe a horizontal bulb of icing, add two more bulbs, one to each side of the first, and repeat.

14. With tube 5 you can achieve larger border variations: a horizontal row of single dots, a reverse shell-motion bulb border and a simple shell-motion bulb border. All are suitable for top or base borders.

15. A fast and easy tube 6 border starts with a zigzag line, to which dots of icing are piped in each curve.

16. Here's a variation on the triple shell border using tube 6. First pipe a horizontal line. Then pipe shell-motion icing bulbs above, below and finally on top of guideline.

17. Another fleur-de-lis border, this time with writing tube 6, makes a perfect trim, large enough for a wedding cake.

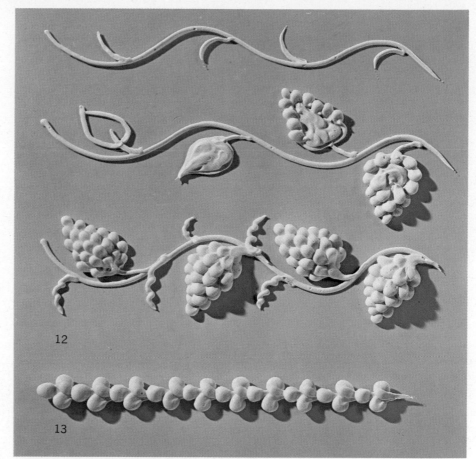

12

13

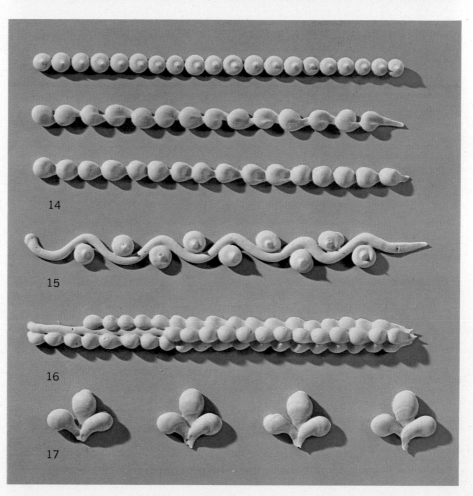

14

15

16

17

MORE WAYS TO MAKE CAKES SPECIAL

An easy way to add importance to any cake is to give it height. Each of the four 10″ cakes on page 147 is given a lift with the 6″ top tier. This provides only six more party servings, but a wealth of decorating possibilities. More height and drama are given by the candles, bassinet and star bouquet. These are quick, easy touches, but they make the difference between just a pretty cake, and one that is impressive. The bouquet and bassinet make nice take-home favors for the guest of honor too. Dream up your own top-knots for cakes—and take advantage of the many charming novelties available.

Candles always add festivity and life to a centerpiece cake. Don't save them just for birthdays—any occasion is made more memorable by candle-light. Candles come in many colors to match or complement your icing. It's a good idea to keep a stock on hand ready to enhance your cakes.

"STAGE" YOUR CAKES

If you are making a cake for an "at-home" party, you have a perfect opportunity to display it in just the right setting. Center the cake on the table and choose table linens and china to set it off. You can keep the tablecloth in a blending color—pale yellow with a yellow, daisy trimmed cake—or make a strong contrast—deep rose for a cake trimmed in tints of pink, or apple green for a lavendar cake. Just be sure the table linens are not so busily patterned that they compete with the decorating details of the cake. An inexpensive sheet given a new hem makes an excellent table cloth when you want to have just the right color for your table.

Surround the cake with low candles set on the cake board—or let the cake rise on a pedestal stand and set taller candles on either side of it.

We have found that cakes lavishly trimmed with icing flowers look best without real flowers on the table.

Cakes that are primarily decorated with borders, or other icing details are set off by the color and grace of real flowers. Try setting such a cake between flowers arranged in two tall compotes or stemmed glasses. Or wreath the cake with long-lasting foliage and just a few fresh flowers.

If you don't have just the right cake stand or tray for your cake, a cardboard cake board will be your choice. These are musts for cakes you sell or give away, too. Cover the cake board in a harmonizing color foil (available at florist supply or florist shops). Tuk-N-Ruffle gives a frilly, dainty look to cakes too.

Just remember—your skillfully decorated cake is a work of art. Give it the right frame and setting.

HOW TO MIX COLORS

Many of our readers have asked us how we mix colors for icings used on our photographed cakes. Here is a listing of most-used colors—some of which are not mixed at all, but taken right from the jar or bottle.

All the colors named are available through the Wilton Yearbook.

BLUE: Royal Blue gives a true or flag blue, with less color a powder blue. Sky blue has a slight aqua tint. Add a trace of Lemon Yellow to Sky Blue for a true aqua.

GOLD COLOR: Add a speck of violet to Golden Yellow.

CHOCOLATE COLOR: Brown plus a little Golden Yellow.

RED: Christmas Red is bright and somewhat lighter than Red-Red. For a deep red, use Red-Red mixed with Christmas Red.

VIOLET: Violet gives a true violet color. In small amounts you will achieve lavendar. Mix it with Royal Blue for a blue-violet. Grape makes a red-violet icing. Small amounts produce orchid. Mix Pink and Royal Blue for a good violet color also.

FLESH COLOR: Add a trace of pink to Copper. For a sun-tan effect, add a trace of Brown to Copper.

GREEN: Leaf Green is used for most leaves. Kelly Green is a cooler green and is used for evergreen needles, or wherever a more blue-green is desired. For an avocado color, use Moss Green. For a yellow green, use Lemon Lime.

PINK: Use Pink in varying amounts for the depth of color you desire.

CORAL: Watermelon gives a fine coral.

SALMON: Use Pink with a speck of Orange.

ORANGE: Use Orange. Add a little Christmas Red for red-orange. Add a little Golden Yellow for yellow-orange.

YELLOW: For a cool, clean yellow, use Lemon Yellow. For a warm golden yellow use Golden Yellow.

RUST: Add specks of Christmas Red and Copper to Orange.

SILVER: Not practical to mix in icing. Use artificial leaves or accessories instead.

For a deep color, buttercream icing is the best to use, but royal icing can also be used. Mix the color with the icing to a medium tint, then fill a paper cone that has been completely painted on the inside with the same hue of paste color. Make the icing a day or two ahead of time—the color deepens as the icing rests. Use as stiff an icing as possible for deep colors—the color tends to thin the icing.

All colors of icing tend to deepen slightly as they dry.

THE MINIMUM PALETTE

If you are a novice decorator, the colors you will find essential for attractive decorating effects are the primary colors—Christmas Red, Lemon Yellow, Royal Blue. Any two of these will combine in varying amounts to give you many more hues. If you combine all three you will produce a drab brown.

A more expanded and convenient palette would contain Leaf Green, Lemon Yellow, Golden Yellow, Royal Blue, Violet, Christmas Red and Orange. By mixing two of these colors together you should be able to achieve almost any hue you want.

Most decorators, however, prefer to have at hand as many colors as possible. Many colors cut down on the time needed for experimenting and make your work easier and faster. Colors are cleaner, too.

If you would like to know more about effects and techniques of color, see The Wilton Way of Cake Decorating, Volume I.

MAKERS of AMERICA

IRELAND
Shown on page 29

A wedding cake spectacular, touched with the fresh green of Ireland's Shamrocks.

Bake and assemble the tiers according to the diagram below. The ornament within the pillars is a tiny Cherub Fountain. Ice in a creamy "Beleek white" buttercream. Make shamrocks with tubes 102 and 103 (directions on page 90) and set aside to dry.

> Blossom Pan Cake
> 5" x 2" round (mini tier)
> 6" Separator plates
> 5" Grecian Pillars
> 10" Bevel Top Pan
> 10" x 3" round
> 12" Bevel Top Pan
> 12" x 3" round
> 16" Base Bevel

Support cake with dowels inserted from lower Separator plate to base of 10" cake (set on cardboard). Insert more dowels in 12" base cake to support tiers above.

To decorate, first measure lines for diamond latticework on each bevel and mark with toothpick. Do two bottom tiers of latticework with tube 4, and make 5-dot flowers at each crossing of lines. Do top bevel and top tier in the same way with tube 2. Pipe tube 6 bulb border around bottom of 12" and 10" cakes, and around plate that holds pillars. Pipe tube 6 bulbwork around base of 5" cake. Mark scallops around sides of each tier and outline with tube 4 dots on top tier. Pipe a border of tube 2 beadwork around base of Blossom cake, and a row of tube 2 stylized shamrocks around top of 5" cake.

Now secure clusters of shamrocks to cake with icing, making a cascade of green. Attach some shamrocks to Cherub Fountain with icing and cluster some at top of Blossom cake around Doves.

AFRICA
shown on page 34

Bake, ice and assemble two tiers, 12" x 4" square and 6" x 2" round. Prick patterns on tier tops. Use tube 4 to outline patterns, then fill in triangle areas below 6" tier with tube 13 stars. Pipe arches on side of 12" tier with tube 5 and drape tube 3 string within them. If icing designs are a little uneven, this will only add to the "hand-crafted" effect. Tube 8 is used for large dots on top of both tiers. Finish with bulb borders: on square tier, tube 12 at base, tube 9 at top. Use tube 8 for borders on 6" tier. Serves 42.

THE AMERICAN INDIAN
shown on page 34

This colorful Thunderbird cake is cut out from a 10" x 3" square cake. After shaping cake according to patter outline, ice thickly with buttercream.

Transfer pattern to grease-proof paper, lay on top of cake and prick design onto top. Outline all areas in beige with tube 2, then fill in with tube 16 stars. Extend stars down sides of cake. Pipe tube 4 eye. Serves about 15.

HOLLAND shown on page 35

First make five tulips, using technique shown on page 72, *1974 Wilton Yearbook* and on page 143, *The Wilton Way*. Pipe long leaves with tube 70 and dry.

The shoe shape is carved from a loaf cake, and is about 10" x 4" overall. (Bake the cake in a Long Loaf pan.) Chill cake, then trim to point at front, curve at back. Indent slightly at base between "heel" and "sole". Hollow out open area to hold tulips. Ice smoothly.

Transfer Delft pattern to grease-proof paper, prick onto cake. Outline pattern with thinned icing, using a tightly rolled paper cone, no tube. Flow in leaf and flower areas. Pipe a thick mound of icing at back of shoe and arrange tulips and leaves. Serves about 8.

ISRAEL
shown on page 38

THE IDEA for this striking Star of David cake was given to us by **Karen Cvetko** of Northbrook, Illinois. Karen trims two round cakes into hexagon shapes, then cuts one cake from point to point into triangles. The triangles are placed against the sides of the second cake to form a six-pointed star. For convenience, we baked two 2-layer cakes in 9" Hexagon Pans. We then cut one cake into six triangles, just as Karen did, and iced the triangles to the sides of the second hexagon cake. We followed Karen's directions for the top ornament, and her ideas for decorating the cake in traditional blue and gold.

First make top ornament to allow plenty of time for drying. Tape CELEBRATE! II pattern to board and tape wax paper over it. Outline the pieces (one whole star and two half stars) in white using tube 2. Then, using same tube, fill in with a gold lace design similar to cornelli, but letting curves of icing touch as much as possible. When thoroughly dry, ice florist wire to lower points of whole and half stars. Edge stars with beading using tube 2. Dry again.

Lay whole star on flat surface, pipe a line of icing down center and position one half star on it, propping with cotton balls until dry. Now push wires into a block of styrofoam, pipe a line of icing on other side of whole star and press on second half star. Hold for a few minutes to set, and dry, propped with cotton balls. When 3-dimensional star is dry, twist wires together and push into a half-ball of styrofoam, flattening the wires underneath. Cover ball with tube 16 stars and set aside while you decorate the cake.

Mark top of cake with pattern and mark sides into triangles. Fill in areas with tube 2 lace work, the same as in the center ornament. Outline lace areas with tube 16 shells. Pipe tube 21 shell border at base of cake. Pipe a few dots of icing on top of cake and position ornament. Edge base of ornament with tube 16 shells. Serves 24.

FRANCE
shown on page 49

The first French to settle in the then not-yet-United States were a brave band of Huguenots who fled religious persecution to settle in South Carolina. Longfellow in his poem "Evangeline", described the plight of the French Arcadians who were driven from Nova Scotia and found a new home in Louisiana, in 1755. French language, food and customs are predominent today in New Orleans.

During the American Revolution, the Marquis de Lafayette, age 20, arrived in America with a party of soldiers in 1777, joined Washington's staff as a major-general and led troops at Brandywine, Gloucester, and Virginia. He later assisted in negotiations that won American Independence. Earth from Bunker Hill covers his grave in Paris.

AS TRIBUTE to French Americans, this simple cake is adorned with the white iris, the fleur-de-lis of France. Directions for making it in icing are on page 90.

The cake is made in two round tiers, 12" x 4" and 8" x 4". All shell borders are done with tube 352, using varying pressure so that borders are larger at bottom, smaller at top. Stylized iris (fleur-de-lis) are piped with tube 5 in shell motion and finished with tube 3 lines and and dots. Attach wired leaves and flowers to side of cake with icing. Serves 98 wedding guests.

CHINA
shown on page 85

A cake that derives its beauty from the art of old China—glowing color, pagoda-like forms and the flowing dragon figure.

Use CELEBRATE! II patterns and do all trims for top and side of cake first. Outline red bars at top of cake with tube 1 and flow in with softened Color Flow icing. Outline red "key designs" with tube 3 and flow in colors so they lie flat as possible. When dry, overpipe outside edges with tube 1 to define shape. Outline dragon with tube 1 and flow in. The cornelli-like "screen" behind dragon is piped with tube 3. Outline shape, then fill in with jiggly lines, making sure lines touch. Pipe gold bars and balls with tube 12 and figure-piping method. Let all dry thoroughly.

Now bake and ice a 9" x 13" x 3" cake and pipe tube 6 ball border around base. Carefully peel wax paper off "cornelli" screen, and place it on top of cake. Next position gold bars and balls. Now trim sugar cubes to height of gold bars and set dragon on cubes. Pipe small mounds of icing to support "key designs" and red bars and position these on cake. Serves 24.

SCOTLAND
shown on page 116

We trimmed this cake with the crest of the Argyle & Sutherland Scottish Regiment, with its dainty thistle design, but any Scottish coat of arms would do as well.

Make the crest first, using pattern and Color Flow technique. Be sure each color is dry before adding next. Make thistle leaves in Color Flow, too, drying on Flower Formers. Make the thistles according to directions in Green Boutique, page 90. Pipe tassels with tubes 2 and 4, just as for "ITALY" below. Set all aside to dry.

Bake and ice a 8" x 3" square cake. Pipe five curving stems on top of cake with tube 16. Tie the stems with a rope made with tube 3. Attach thistles to ends of stems with icing. Add leaves, attaching with dots of icing. Attach tassels to ends of rope with icing.

Pipe a tube 19 shell border around base of cake. Carefully prop crest against cake on mounds of icing. Serves 12.

SPAIN
shown on page 117

With a lacy mantilla, a tortoiseshell comb, and deep red roses, this dainty cake calls up romantic images of the dark-eyed beauties of Spain.

Make the comb first using pattern and Color Flow. Tape wax paper over the pattern on 10" cake-side formers and outline with tube 1, flowing in very thin tan icing. When dry dab with cloth dipped in copper-tinted water. Pipe tube 1 "pearls".

Bake and ice a two-layer oval cake. Now make lace ruffle. Take 4' length of white nylon tulle and cut strip 1½" wide. Cut scallops along one side and run needle and thread along straight side, ready to be gathered. Working with about 6" of net at a time, pipe tube 1 lace design, following pattern. Apply tube 1 red zigzag to scalloped edge. Gather each section into ruffle while still wet. When finished, ruffle will be about 2' long. Tie thread or secure with icing.

Now ice cake with ecru buttercream and pipe tube 18 shell border around bottom. Place ruffle on cake, secure with icing. Transfer lace pattern to cake with pin. Pipe with tube 1, cover cake with tube 1 lattice, then over-pipe lace pattern. Pipe tube 2 beading to cover inner edge of ruffle. Serves 12.

DENMARK
shown on page 118

A stunning picture of colorful Viking ships at sea!

Make the Color Flow picture in two sections—the sky with rising sun and sea, and the foreground with ships and more sea, using CELEBRATE! II pattern. Dry.

Bake and ice a 9" x 13" x 3" cake. Pipe mounds of icing on top of cake and position sky portion of Color Flow. Pipe higher mounds to support ship section. Then pipe rigging on ships with tube 1. Pipe tube 14 shells to frame picture. Pipe top border on cake with tube 19, base with tube 21. Serves 24.

ITALY
shown on page 119

The Pinta, the Nina and the Santa Maria sail to the New World!

Make the three ships in advance, using Color Flow technique and patterns. Outline with tube 1, fill in and set aside to dry. To make the tassels, pipe a ball of icing with tube 4 on wax paper. Pull out three lines of icing from ball with tube 2 to establish width and length of fringe. Add tube 2 lines in layers until shape is achieved. Bind top of fringe with three lines of tube 2 string, just below ball. Dry.

Bake a 6" ball cake and a 10" x 4" square cake. Trim bottom of ball cake to flatten slightly and set on 5½" separator plate from round Mini-Tier Set. Clip legs of separator plate to 4". Ice ball cake, and referring to globe, mark shapes of continents with a toothpick. Pat water areas with damp sponge for stucco effect and fill in land with tube 16 stars.

Ice square cake smoothly. Pipe tube 104 tri-color swags at corners. Pipe tube 2 beading and attach tassels with icing. Push legs of separator plate (with ball cake on top) into top of cake. Heap boiled icing on top and swirl with spatula for cloud effect. Set ships in position with icing and pipe tube 2 swirls for waves. Finish square cake with tube 11 bulb borders. Serves 32.

GERMANY
(The Night before Christmas)

shown on page 129

Almost seven million Germans have emigrated to the United States, starting in 1683 when 13 German families arrived in Pennsylvania to live peaceably according to their religious beliefs. Since then, wave after wave of their countrymen have come, to flee regligious persecution and to find freedom. Many became prosperous farmers in the midwest states. One of their special gifts to America has been the enrichment of the Christmas celebration.

The whole family will enjoy making this typically German gingerbread house.

Since it is a sizeable project, break it down into several evenings of work.

BEFORE YOU BEGIN. Have on hand ingredients for marzipan, gingerbread, royal and boiled icing. Purchase lollipops and candies for trim. Prepare a 20"x 20" board for base—plywood or four thicknesses of corrugated board taped together. Cover with foil.

1. MAKE SANTA, Mrs. Santa, Klick and other elves in marzipan according to directions on page 96. Figures should dry at least 48 hours. Make Christmas trees on Cone Formers or ice cream cones and pipe with tube 74, starting at base.

2. BAKE GINGERBREAD. Make two recipes for enough for house and yard and cookie trims. After you have cut out the larger pieces, use remainder of dough for crescent, heart and star-shaped cookies and ¼" strips to make balcony. (Any extras will be eaten on the spot!) Here is Chef Olkiewicz's delicious recipe.

GINGERBREAD

8 ounces sugar
pinch of salt
1½ pounds honey
3½ ounces lard
2¼ pounds flour
½ pound coarsely chopped almonds
½ teaspoon gingebread spice
3 teaspoons cinnamon
2 eggs
3 teaspoons water
1 ounce baking soda

Mix sugar, salt, honey and lard in a saucepan and heat until blended (about 110-115 degrees); do not allow it to boil. Remove from heat and cool in the refrigerator. Place flour, almonds and spices in large mixing bowl. Make a well in center of flour and pour in honey mixture, eggs, and baking soda dissolved in water. Mix together well, working flour from outside into

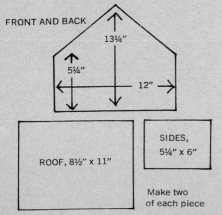

FRONT AND BACK

13¼"

5¼"

12"

ROOF, 8½" x 11"

SIDES,
5¼" x 6"

Make two
of each piece

center. Knead dough lightly, then let it rest in refrigerator at least 2 hours.

Roll out dough on lightly floured board and cut out house pieces according to diagram with a sharp knife. Cut a 18" x 18" piece for base. Cut ¼" strips for balcony. Use rest to cut out cookies for trim. To tranfer large pieces to buttered jelly-roll pans dusted with flour, take a cardboard circle larger than the piece of dough and dust it with a little flour. Lift edge of dough with spatula, slide cardboard under it, then slide it gently into the pan. Leave space between pieces, as gingerbread will spread during baking. Bake in a 375-400 degree oven for about 25-30 minutes, or until firm and lightly browned. After 20 minutes of baking, check to make sure it is not too brown, and remove if done.

3. ASSEMBLE. All pieces are assembled with Royal Icing. To support walls while you work, use clean #2 cans. Put base on board. First, pipe royal icing around sides and back wall, and put these together, propping with cans on the inside of the house. Allow time for each piece to set firmly. Cut door and window openings before you put up front wall. Remove cans from inside house, then attach front wall. Let dry thoroughly.

To attach roof, place both sections upside-down on work table, and pipe royal icing around all sides. Join top seams together, then pick up the complete roof, using both hands, and invert it over the wall opening. Hold in place for about 5 minutes until you feel it has set enough not to slide off. Have two small cans or cups nearby, to slide under ends of roof when you let go. These must support it for at least 30 minutes.

4. DECORATE. Tint royal icing and thin to "paint" cookies. Trim with tube 2 dots. Build balcony from gingerbread strips, attach above door with toothpicks and royal icing. Trim with tube 13. Make wreath with tube 65, add tube 3 berries. Attach cookies and candies to house. Heap boiled icing "snow" on roof and yard and sprinkle with edible glitter. Make a "path" with a spatula and pave with candies. Place lollipop fence and trees in position. Heap "snow" on trees. Now put the marzipan people in the front yard. Klick will need royal icing and toothpicks to hold in place. Pipe tube 12 ball border all around.

This gingerbread Christmas scene will keep for years if stored in a cool, dry place.

SWEDEN
shown on page 133

Let this charming doll cake be the centerpiece for Christmas morning breakfast.

Cut a 2" ring of ½" thick styrofoam for her wreath. Insert plastic candle holders, then cover with tube 65 leaves. Cover star pattern with wax paper, place a straight pin on one point of star with point extending below it. Then outline and flow in star

with Color Flow technique. (Pin will attach star to doll's head.) Make tiny lace hearts by taping wax paper over pattern and piping with tube 1.

Bake a Wonder Mold cake and ice as smoothly as possible with shiny boiled icing. Insert doll pick and cover bodice and arms with tube 16 stars. Add tube 1 "pearls" at neck. Pipe a tube 16 shell border around base of skirt, above it a tube 103 drape, then tube 2 string. Attach lace hearts at points of string with dots of icing. Attach ribbon bow at waist with icing.

Place wreath carefully on doll's head, push in star and insert candles. Serves 12.

JAPAN
shown on page 140

A dainty tableau with a miniature bridge crossing a peaceful stream.

Make the cherry blossoms according to the directions on page 90. The "shoji screen" on the sides is made in four pieces with Color Flow technique and pattern.

Now for the bridge—a real engineering feat. The floor portion is done in three sections, two with eight "planks" and one with six planks. Tape pattern to 8" Cake-side former, tape wax paper over, and outline planks with tube 1. Flow in and dry thoroughly. Do two railings. Tape pattern to board, cover with wax paper and outline complete pattern with tube 1. Then flow in. When dry, turn over, outline again *down to lower arched rail only*. Flow in and dry. Set one railing upright, with the side where lower arch is not flowed facing in. Pipe tube 2 line of icing just below vertical rails on this side. Set three floor pieces snugly against this line. Repeat for second railing. Prop to dry, then reinforce with icing under side of "floor" where pieces join. You will have achieved a perfect, sturdy, little arched bridge.

Bake and ice a 10" x 4" square cake. Cover top with green icing, leaving space for "stream." Pat with damp sponge to simulate grass. Fill stream area with tinted piping gel. Set Color Flow screens against sides, attaching with dots of icing. Pipe tube 21 shell borders. Pipe tube 3 stems and place cherry blossoms, adding tube 65 leaves.

Set the little bridge above the stream and trim the cake with dainty paper parasols. Serves 20.

RUSSIA
shown on page 141

To decorate this lovely Swan Lake cake, cover CELEBRATE! II patterns with wax paper, outline with tube 2 and fill in with Color Flow. When dry, figure-pipe Color Flow swan body on both sides with tube 3 for three dimensional effect, then pipe tube 101s "feathers" on Color Flow wings. Attach wings with icing and add more tube 101s feathers to body, piping swan's crown, eyes and beak with tube 1.

For the cake, ice and assemble a 12" x 4" round and a 6" x 3" petal with 8" separator plates and 5" Corinthian pillars. Outline the reverse colonial scroll borders on the tier sides with a toothpick; then overpipe outlines, feathering scroll ends and flowering centers, using tube 21 for the 12" tier, tube 16 for the 6" tier. Add tiny blue branch trims to scrolls with tubes 1 and 2.

Now edge separator plate with tube 16; then pipe shell-and-scroll top and base borders around both tiers using tube 18. To finish, position Dancing Ballerinas around 12" tier top, framing figurine bases with tube 16, and place swan atop cake. Serves 76, beautiful enough for a stunning wedding cake.

POLAND
shown on page 142

Pretty folk dancers in a field of flowers celebrate the proud heritage of Poland. The colorful side trim is adapted from generations-old Polish needlework.

First make dancers with Color Flow icing and pattern. Cover pattern with wax paper and tape to cardboard. Outline with tube 1 and flow in colors. When dry, peel off paper and flow in back for extra strength. When pieces are thoroughly dry, decorate with tube 1 hair, features, beads, stripes on skirts and other details. Pipe tube 101s white ruffle at edge of one skirt.

Next bake and ice a 10"x4" round cake. Draw around 8" cake circle with toothpick to position crescent of flowers. Thin royal icing to mayonnaise consistency and pipe tube 1 flowers, freehand, of dots in various sizes. Taper the flowers from large in center to very small at tips of crescent. For design around side of cake, use pattern and pipe tube 2 lines and dots. Pipe tube 7 ball border around base and top of cake. Pipe small mounds of icing to support dancer at right, and set the other one slightly higher on sugar cubes trimmed to size. Their boots should project over the flowers. Serves 14.

CHRISTMAS CANDY (continued)
shown on page 131
Filling
      6 ounces butter
      6 ounces fondant
    12 ounces tempered dark chocolate
      5 ounces cherry brandy

Mix butter and fondant together as for buttercream. Gradually whip in chocolate and cherry brandy. Fill paper cone fitted with tube 19 and drop filling onto rounds to form little mountains. Refrigerate. Dip into dark chocolate, and when this coating has cooled, dip tip of candy into milk chocolate for decorative effect.

MOCHA HALF-MOONS
      8 ounces almond paste
   1½ ounces confectioners sugar
      1 ounce Kahlua liqueur
      1 teaspoon instant coffee powder
      tempered chocolate for dipping
      pre-molded milk chocolate hearts

Mix first four ingredients thoroughly and form into small crescent shaped pieces about the size of a teaspoon. Let dry 20 minutes. Dip with bent fork into tempered chocolate and harden on wax paper. Place a milk chocolate heart on each, secured with a dot of soft chocolate.

WALNUT RUM STARS
      8 ounces almond paste
      2 ounces confectioners sugar
      2 ounces chopped toasted walnuts
      2 tablespoons rum
      tempered dark chocolate for dipping
      pre-molded chocolate stars for trim

Mix first four ingredients, roll out about ½" thick on board dusted with confectioners sugar and cut into squares, tidbits or other shapes. Let dry and dip into chocolate with bent fork. Top with chocolate star secured with dot of soft chocolate.

THE FIRST THANKSGIVING
shown on page 134

Prepare the Color Flow pieces in advance, and then you can assemble this gala holiday centerpiece in a jiffy.

Use CELEBRATE! II pattern for top, and two sections of top pattern for sides. Make four each of the side trims (a total of eight). Outline patterns with tube 1 and flow in colors thickly for puffy effect. When pieces are thoroughly dry, overpipe designs to emphasize details. Pipe fringe on Indian costume with tube 2, pipe stems with tube 1s, leaves with 65s, watermelon seeds with tube 1. Paint stripes on gourds and brush a little color on men's cheeks with small artist's brush.

Bake and ice a 12" x 4" two-layer square cake. Attach color Flow side pieces to corners with dots of icing. Position top piece on small mounds of icing, or on flat sugar cubes. Pipe tube 19 shell border around base. Serves 30.

CUPID OFF HIS PEDESTAL
shown on page 121

A variation on the more formal Mexican style of decorating, this charming cake shows Cupid stepping down from his pedestal to dance amid the flowers.

First make Color Flow butterflies and disc for top of cake. Tape wax paper over patterns. Outline the butterflies with tube 1 and flow in color; when dry decorate with tube 1 dots. Outline disc with tube 2 and flow in Color Flow icing; when dry, cover with tube 1 cornelli.

In advance, make lots of tube 103 roses and rosebuds, and tube 66 leaves. Make small daisies with tube 103 petals and tube 4 centers sprinkled with glitter. Mount all on florist wire. Pipe lots of tube 352 leaves and mount on wires; tape several wires together to make branches, then combine branches into a bush.

Bake and ice a 4" high oval cake, set off-center on foil-covered board. Pin wax paper pattern to side of cake and draw curved line with toothpick. Ice top portion green and pat for stucco effect. Cover white portion with white tube 1 cornelli work. Pipe tube 4 bead border along dividing line and tube 9 white ball border around bottom of cake. Set disc on top of cake and pipe tube 4 green beading around it. Set Decorator Base on disc and arrange flowers, leaves and butterflies. Position Dancing Cupid on mound of icing and arrange leaves and daisy around his feet. Serves 12.

THE THANKSGIVING TURKEY
shown on page 135

A stylized version of America's favorite Thanksgiving feast!

Make the turkey first. Tape pattern to board and tape wax paper over. Sugar-mold breast in half of a 3" egg mold and place on the wax paper. Now pipe tube 104 "feathers", starting with tail and piping over breast. Figure-pipe neck and head with tube 6. Add "wattle" with tube 4. Now pipe six "fans" of feathers to go around sides of cake, using pattern. Let dry.

Make wheat in advance, following directions in "The Green Boutique", page 90. When dry, make two bundles of six stalks each, wire together and tie with gold cord.

Bake, ice and assemble a 12" x 3" hexagon cake and an 8" x 2" round cake. Pipe a tube 17 shell border at base of round cake. Secure "fans" to sides of hexagon cake with icing, then pipe a tube 18 zigzag border at base with upright shell at each corner. Lay bundles of wheat on cake. Pipe a big mound of icing on top of cake and position turkey. Carry proudly to the table to serve 25.

Continued from *page 104*

is held against the body and holds a twig "fishing rod" and the other is out-stretched to hold a "fish" shaped from left-over cake. Feet are cut off too, and turned to make the figure "walk". As a final touch, more left-over cake is made into a jumping "frog" near his leg.

Mrs. Dean Stout, Cameron, Missouri, made two cute "look alike" cakes for her twin sons on their third birthday. The cakes were "dressed" in replicas of the boys' sweaters and pants and each wore a gay party hat. Color of hair and eyes were matched to that of the birthday boys.

Ann Tudyk, San Antonio, Texas, created an astronaut standing on the moon for her 4-year old nephew. "I baked the cake with your doll pan and a 12″ round pan. I cut a portion out of the round cake to insert the feet of the other. After I iced the moon, I used the bottom of a glass to create the craters." The astronaut's suit was covered with tube 17 stars with tube 7 used for the arms and legs. He holds an American flag piped with tubes 7 and 14.

Denise Verhagen of Appleton, Wisconsin, shapes her cake into a "gentleman at leisure" wearing corduroy trousers (tube 47) and a tweedy jacket (tube 27). She adds a little plastic pipe.

Chris Wilson, Starke, Florida, decorated a neat looking cowboy all in stars. She used a kidney-shaped piece of cardboard for his broad-brimmed hat and covered that with stars, too.

Mrs. Ivan Jensen, Hays, Kansas, makes another cowboy, wearing red striped shirt, boots and holsters.

Faye Keitel, Shawnee Mission, Kansas, shares a neat state trooper, leaving the skirt extension on the cake and icing it as two holsters. The hat brim is formed of a Twinkie, cut in half.

Glenda Lattin, Jerome, Idaho, ices the rag doll like a football player, complete with striped jersey and helmet.

Donna Franssen, Pine Ridge, South Dakota, decorated a "policeman" cake for a policeman friend. He is neatly covered with stars, with "silver" shields on hat and shirt made of foil.

Arlene Evans, Waretown, N. J., decorates her doll cake as George Washington, our first Commander-in-Chief. He wears blue and tan uniform, white wig and Revolutionary-style hat.

ICE CARVING BASICS

After seeing Mr. Mizuuchi's brilliant creation on page 14, many decorating enthusiasts will want to attempt this unique and fascinating art. Here is a brief list of basics for the beginner.

WORK AREA: You will need a cool area with room to move around. A basement or garage make excellent work locations. The temperature of your work area should be somewhere between a few degrees above freezing and 50° F to allow adequate carving time. This is a winter project!

In addition to the proper location, you will need a sturdy table on which to work and a catchall for the melting ice. An 8 or 10 foot diameter plastic wading pool makes an excellent container. Or construct a woden frame with 8′ x 6″ boards and drape a large plastic cloth within the frame. Scatter old rugs on the plastic lining to assure sound footage as the ice melts.

WORK TOOLS: Mr. Mizuuchi, and other professionals, use more elaborate and costly tools than a beginner needs. His basic tool kit consists of an ice pick, 7 chisels with handles long enough to provide leverage, 2 "V" shaped chisels, a coarse-toothed saw with a blade approximately 2 feet long and a smaller saw which resembles the kind used for light tree pruning.

A much simpler assortment will suffice for the beginner: an ice pick, a sturdy 5-pronged fork, a chisel of 1″ width and a "V"-shaped chisel in which each side of the "V" is ½ inch. A saw about 2 feet long and with the very coarse teeth used on logs is a big help in quickly cutting large chunks of ice from the block, but this job can be done with the chisel and fork. All tools should be of good quality with strong wooden handles.

THE ICE: For your first ice carving project, a 50 lb. or 100 lb. block is best, nothing smaller or larger. The ice should be clear, without flaws or discolorations. When you order the ice, specify it is for a carving project.

Naturally the ice can be stored in the freezer, before and after carving; however you will need a strong helper to transport it. Before you position the ice on your work table, place the block on a folded towel set in a large pan.

CLOTHING: Wear a heavy sweater, boots and work gloves.

BEFORE YOU START:

1. BE SURE to have a diagram, preferably enlarged to full size, of the design you are planning to carve.

2. DON'T chip too much ice off at one time. Take small chips so you can continually check your progress.

3. DON'T exercise too much force on the ice as you near completion of your carving. Once the basic shape is refined, the ice is more fragile and easily susceptible to cracks or fractures.

4. DON'T become discouraged if your first attempt at ice carving is not successful. Simply let it melt and resolve that your next carving will be a masterpiece.

BASKET DIAGRAM

To carve the spectacular basket of ice on page 14, Mr. Mizuuchi used a 100 lb. block, 21″ high x 18″ wide x 9″ thick.

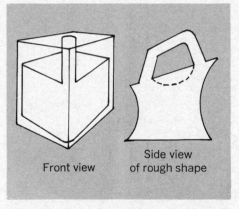

Front view

Side view of rough shape

Note how the basket sits diagonally within the block of ice. In the side view, observe how basket and handle slant down. Dotted lines indicate where bowl is hollowed out.

THE CARVING DISPLAY

A few props are needed to display your beautiful sculpture. Set a large flat-bottomed bowl or metal pan on the serving table. Place a folded towel in it. Now, holding the basket just above the base, carry it from the freezer to the table. Conceal the pan or bowl with foliage. Fill the basket with fresh fruit. Your creation will normally last for a full three hours.

NOTE: If you are unable to acquire any ice carving tools in your area write to:
    FROG Tool Co., Ltd.
    548 North Wells
    Chicago, Illinois 60610

FROG will be glad to provide you with costs and other information.

HOW TO CUT A CAKE

In response to many queries from our readers, here are cutting guides for cakes of all sizes and shapes. Keep in mind that wedding cakes are cut in small, sample-sized pieces—party cakes more generously. We've added a handy baking-and-batter guide.

WEDDING CAKE CUTTING GUIDE

The procedure for cutting any tiered cake, regardless of shape, is basically the same. The first step is to remove the top tier, and then begin the cutting with the second tier followed by third, fourth and so on. The top tier can also be cut, but often it is saved for a later celebration.

To cut round tiers, move in two inches from the tier's outer edge, cut a circle and then slice one inch pieces within circle. Now move in another two inches, cut another circle, slice one-inch pieces and so on until the tier is completely cut. The center core of each tier and the small top tier can be cut into halves, quarters, sixths, eighths, depending on size.

To cut square tiers, move in two inches from the tier's outer edge and cut across. Then slice one inch pieces of cake. Now move in another two inches and slice again until the entire tier is cut.

Cut petal-shaped tiers similar to round tiers as diagram shows.

Cut hexagon tiers similar to round tiers.

To cut heart-shaped cake tiers, divide the tiers vertically into halves, quarters, sixths or eighths. Within rows, slice one inch pieces of cake.

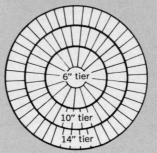

Top view of a three-tiered round cake

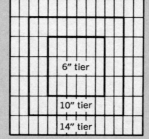

Top view of a three-tiered square cake

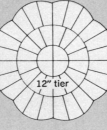

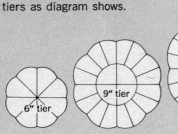

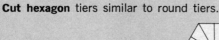

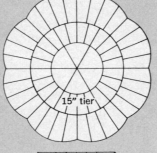

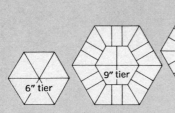

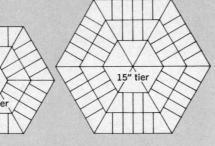

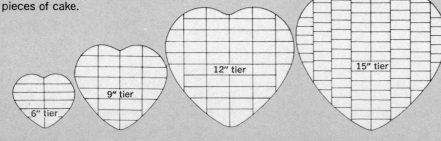

WEDDING CAKE SERVING CHART

Following the tier cake cutting procedures at left, here's an approximation of the number of servings you can expect from each cake tier.

SHAPE	SIZE	SERVINGS
ROUND	6"	16
	8"	30
	10"	48
	12"	68
	14"	92
	16"	118
	18"	148
SQUARE	6"	18
	8"	32
	10"	50
	12"	72
	14"	98
	16"	128
	18"	162
HEXAGON	6"	6
	9"	22
	12"	50
	15"	66
PETAL	6"	8
	9"	20
	12"	44
	15"	62
HEART	6"	12
	9"	28
	12"	48
	15"	90

PARTY CAKE SERVING CHART

Unlike tiered cakes which are conservatively cut to serve large groups, party cakes are cut into more generous portions. Here is an approximation of the number of servings you can expect from each. One-mix cakes, of any shape, serve twelve.

SHAPE	SIZE	SERVINGS
ROUND	6"	6
	8"	10
	10"	14
	12"	22
	14"	36
SQUARE	6"	8
	8"	12
	10"	20
	12"	36
	14"	42
RECTANGLE	9"x13"	24
	11"x15"	35
	12"x18"	54
HEART	SIZE	SERVINGS
	6"	6
	9"	12
	12"	24
	15"	35
HEXAGON	6"	6
	9"	12
	12"	20
	15"	48
PETAL	6"	6
	8"	8
	12"	26
	15"	48

PARTY CAKE CUTTING GUIDE

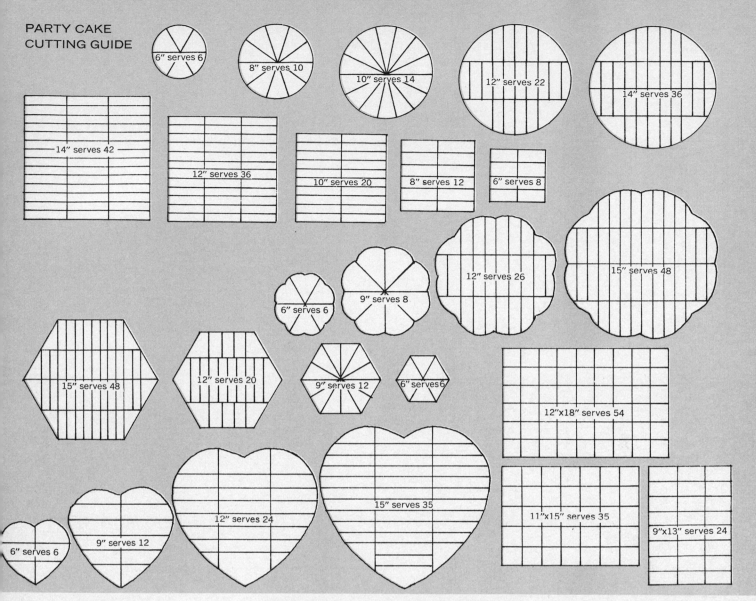

6" serves 6
8" serves 10
10" serves 14
12" serves 22
14" serves 36

14" serves 42
12" serves 36
10" serves 20
8" serves 12
6" serves 8

6" serves 6
9" serves 8
12" serves 26
15" serves 48

15" serves 48
12" serves 20
9" serves 12
6" serves 6
12"x18" serves 54

6" serves 6
9" serves 12
12" serves 24
15" serves 35
11"x15" serves 35
9"x13" serves 24

ONE-CAKE-MIX PANS

The following cakes are all made with pans requiring one standard packaged cake mix or approximately six cups of batter, and each serves approximately 12 guests. For specific baking times, refer to instructions included with the pans.

Bell Set	Lamb
Blossom Set	Loveable Animal
Book Set	Mickey Mouse* and
Bowling Pin	Disney characters
Bunny	Mini-Toy Set
Clown	Oval
Cross	Panda
Egg set	Petal Set—9"
Elephant	Piano
Flag	Poppin' Fresh®
Flower pan	Round Mini-Tier
Fred Flintstone**	Scooby Doo**
Grand Slam Set	Square Tier Set—5"
Guitar	Star
Heart Mini-Tier	Story Book Doll
Hippo	Train
Holly Hobbie™†	Tree Pans
Horseshoe	Wonder Mold
Interchangeable Pan	Yogi Bear**

BATTER AND BAKING CHART

All baking times are for preheated 350° oven.

Pan	Size	Cups of Batter	Baking Time in minutes	Pan	Size	Cups of Batter	Baking Time in minutes
ROUND (2" deep)	6"	2½	25-35	RECTANGLE (2" deep)	9"x13"	8	30-40
	8"	4	30-40		11"x15"	11	30-40
	10"	6	30-40		12"x18"	15	30-40
	12"	9	30-40	BEVEL (Top)	8"	3½	30-40
	14"	11½	30-40		10"	6	30-40
	16"	14	35-45		12"	7½	30-40
	18"	16	35-45	BEVEL (Base)	14"	7	25-35
SQUARE (2" deep)	6"	3	25-35		16"	9	25-35
	8"	4½	30-40	LONG LOAF (4¼" deep)	16"x4"	12 (2 mixes)	55-65
	10"	7	30-40	LITTLE LOAFERS (1½" deep)	4⅜"x2½"	½ cup ea. pan	20-30
	12"	10½	30-40				
	14"	13½	30-40	BALL PAN	6" diam.	2⅓ cups ea. pan half	35-45
	16"	15½	35-45				
	18"	18	35-45	BLOSSOM PANS	4⅝" diam.	¾ cup ea. pan	20-30
PETAL (2" deep)	6"	2	25-35				
	9"	4	30-40	SMALL WONDER MOLDS (3" deep)	3½" diam.	¾ cup ea. mold	20-30
	12"	6½	30-40				
	15"	12	30-40				
HEART (2" deep)	6"	2	25-35				
	9"	4	30-40				
	12"	8½	30-40				
	15"	12	30-40				
HEXAGON (2" deep)	6"	1½	25-35				
	9"	3½	30-40				
	12"	7	30-40				
	15"	12	30-40				

INDEX

AMERICANA CAKES, 60-61, 74-75, 105, 115, 134-135, 139

ANIMAL CAKES
lamb, 36
panda, 57, 111

ANNIVERSARY CAKES, front cover

AUSTRALIAN METHOD OF DECORATING
inspired by, 63
technique, 62

BASKET CAKES, 24-25, 106

BATTER, amount held in pans, 159

BICENTENNIAL CAKES, front cover, 75, 84, 86

BIRTHDAY CAKES, 57, 86, 147

BOOK CAKES, 12-13, 73, 82-83, 143

CANDIES, hand-dipped chocolate, 131

CHRISTMAS
Cakes, 9, 26, 125, 127-128, 132-133, 136, 145, 147
story, 126-130

COLOR-FLOW
cakes trimmed with this method, 20, 60-61, 75, 85-87, 115-118, 130, 134-135, 140-143 (?117, 119)

COLOR, how to use, 146-147, 152

COLORS, how to mix, 152

COOKIES
used in decorating, 22, 37, 40, 110

CORNELLI LACE, cakes trimmed with, 11, 23, 120, 121

CORN, 92

COVERING CAKES
marzipan, 96
mock fondant, 115
rolled fondant, 94

DECORATING FOR PROFIT, 71-72

DOLL CAKES, 26, 87, 111, 133

EASTER
cakes, 28, 30, 31, 33, 36
cupcakes and doughnuts, 41
eggs decorated for, 27

ENGAGEMENT CAKES, 18, 40, 46

ENGLISH METHOD OF CAKE DECORATING, 42, 44
cake inspired by English method, 43

EXTENSION WORK, cakes decorated with, 23, 62-63

FATHER'S DAY CAKES, 60, 64

FLOWERS
cakes trimmed with icing flowers, 11-13, 16-19, 22-23, 25, 28, 30-31, 35, 38-39, 40-43, 46-50, 52-55, 58-59, 62-64, 73, 76, 77, 78-83, 87-88, 110, 112-113, 116, 120-121, 125, 136, 139-140, 142, 143, 147
cakes trimmed with fresh flowers, 51, 56
drop flowers, 16, 22-23, 25, 37, 41, 50, 55, 110, 111
flowers used in decoration,
bellflower, 90
calla lily, 32
cherry blossom, 91
cosmos, 91
dogwood, 93
iris, 92
marsh marigold, 90
mayflower, 92
pompon, 93
pussywillow, 93
shaggy mums, 93
shamrock, 91
spring beauty, 90
sunflower, 93
thistle of Scotland, 91
trillium, 90
zinnia, 90
flowers, mounting on wire, 93

FONDANT
cakes iced with, 62-63
candy made with, 131
petits fours iced with, 115
recipe for, 94, 115, 131

FRUIT
fresh, used in ice basket, 14
marzipan, 24, 106

GINGERBREAD HOUSE, 128-129
gingerbread recipe, 155

GROOM'S CAKE, 53

GUM PASTE
cakes trimmed with, 33, 40, 75, 111, 136
recipe for, 32

HALLOWEEN CAKE, 109

HEART CAKES, 17-20, 22-23, 45, 55, 80

HOLIDAY CAKES
Christmas, 9, 26, 125, 127-130, 132-133, 136, 145, 147
Easter, 28, 30, 31, 33, 36
Fourth of July, front cover, 6, 75, 84, 86-87, 147
Halloween, 109
Hanukah, 137
New Year, 9, 11
Thanksgiving, 26, 105, 134-135

ICE CARVING, 14-15

ICINGS
fondant, Wilton, 131
high humidity buttercream, 104
mock fondant, 115
rolled fondant, 94
royal icing, Mexican, 121

JEWISH MOTIF, cakes decorated with, 38, 137

LACE
cakes trimmed with, 50, 117
cornelli, 11, 23, 120, 121

LATTICE, cakes trimmed with, 13, 17, 23, 40, 46, 53, 55

MAKERS OF AMERICA, cakes saluting Africa, 34; American Indian, 34; China, 85; Denmark, 118; England, 76-77; France, 49; Germany, 129; Holland, 35; Ireland, 29; Israel, 38; Italy, 119; Japan, 140; Poland, 142; Russia, 141; Scotland, 116; Spain, 117; Sweden, 133

MAKERS OF AMERICA CAKES
how to decorate, 77, 153, 155

MARZIPAN
cakes decorated with, 10, 24, 87, 106, 127-128, 144
figures made of, 10, 128-129, 144
fruits and vegetables made of, 24-25, 106
recipe, 96

MEN'S CAKES, 53, 57, 60, 61, 64, 84

MEXICAN CAKES, 120
cakes inspired by Mexican method, 121

MOTHER'S DAY CAKES, 21, 45, 58-59, 64

NUMBER OF SERVINGS OF CAKES, 157-158

PATRIOTIC CAKES, front cover, 6, 12-13, 26, 73, 75, 82-84, 86-87, 143, 147

PETITS FOURS, 115

PRESIDENTS' PORTRAIT CAKES, 12, 13, 73, 82, 83, 143
how to decorate, 65

PULLED SUGAR CAKE, 122, how to make, 123-124

QUICK AND PRETTY CAKES, 23, 40, 64, 137

RECIPES
fondant, 131
gingerbread, 155
gum paste, Mexican, 121
marzipan, 96
mock fondant, 115
rolled fondant, 94
pastillage, 120
royal icing, Mexican, 121

SOUTH AFRICAN CAKE, 88
cake inspired by, 88

STAR METHOD, cakes using, 26, 34, 36-37, 84, 87, 132, 136, 145

TEEN CAKES, 78, 112-113

THANKSGIVING CAKES, 26, 105, 134-135

TIER CAKES
how to cut, 157-158
servings from, 157-158
wedding cakes, (see "Wedding")

VALENTINE'S DAY CAKES, 16-17, 20-23

WEDDING CAKES, 19, 29, 47-52, 54-56, 107, 125

WHEAT SHOCKS, 92

WILDFLOWER CAKES, 30-31